Foundational Leaders

Cornerstones of Successful Strategic Execution

Bob Chapman Ph.D.

To the Point Press

Houston, Texas

Acknowledgements

The content for this book comes from twenty-five years worth of conversations with countless leaders. These conversations were largely "in the midst of battle" of planning and implementing change. A friend who read a pre-publication version of this book said, "This is very good stuff; how did you think it all up?" It was at that point that I realized that I needed to make explicit the acknowledgement that if you perceive there to be "good stuff" in this book, it came from leaders who went before you. While I have woven the learnings from others together, the real value comes from the courage and tenacity of committed business leaders.

To use an analogy, I am like a bee that takes pollen from one flower and flies to fertilize another flower. The bee serves a useful purpose, and yet the value comes from the sharing between the flowers.

I have been blessed to work with countless leaders, so I would like to acknowledge all of those whom have been willing to share their experiences and lives with me. Three stand out as exemplary Foundational Leaders, and I would like to acknowledge them: Joel Staff, Tom Stephens and Chris Wright. Each is a splendid example of foundational commitments at work, and each has been very successful in leading change in multiple companies.

I would also like to acknowledge my writing coach and friend, Elizabeth Neeld. She is remarkable as a writer, coach and friend. I would also like to acknowledge my business partner Kevin Cullen for encouraging me to begin writing again and for working with Elizabeth.

This book is dedicated to Francis Vidal,
Dear friend and colleague who
Lived his life as only Francis could
And is sorely missed by his sons and
Those who knew and loved him.

Table of Contents

The Intent of
To the Point Press

Books Written for People Who Want Practical Advice and Are Often Too Busy To Read

Most of you who will read this book, seldom read management books. You have so much to read for your daily tasks and you are so busy working that you do not take time out of your day to read management books. You also find that much of what is written in management books does not apply to your work. You find that your limited time is better spent doing something else other than reading management books since you get so little value from them. If that sounds like you, this book was written for you.

As challenging or crazy, as it may seem, this is a book written explicitly for people who are too busy to read. That is, people who are busy working and want useful information presented in a manner that is to the point. Hence, I am organizing my writings on strategic execution into a series of short books and calling the series "To the Point".

This first book in the To the Point series focuses on the cornerstone of success for strategic execution: leaders. Leaders make strategic execution successful. I have seen many attempts at strategic execution fail, and invariably at the core of what went wrong was an absence of effective leaders. Further, these efforts were hampered by bad attempts to lead.

When I pick up a book I often start with the question, "Is this the right book for me? How can I know what this book is about and how practical will it be?"

I have written this book for people who seldom read management books. My clients are usually too busy to read much, and seldom read chapter to chapter. Rather they read when time permits and skip around looking for content that matters to them. I have written this for that type of person. I have written each chapter to stand alone. You can get the essence of this book without reading the chapters sequentially.

How to Use to the Point Books

Each book is written to make it easy for you to skip around as well as focus in on what will be most helpful to you given what you are currently facing. I have written each chapter to be:

To the Point Books:
1. Practical
2. Personalized
3. Independent
4. Non-sequential
5. Action-oriented
6. Self-guided
7. Addresses some of the peculiarities of human behavior

1. **Practical**

   Most of the chapter is written directly about what you are likely encountering or will encounter if you are executing strategic change in your business. This is practical advice for someone who is "in the trenches" from someone who has been working with folks "in the trenches" for over 25 years.

2. **Personalized**

   Each chapter is written in a personal, conversational manner. I have intentionally NOT mentioned a lot of names of client companies and executives with whom I have worked. Name dropping is not appropriate in personalized conversations. I hope you experience it as if you and I were sitting in those comfortable chairs in the corner of your neighborhood Starbucks, having a nice coffee and a provocative conversation.

3. Independent

Each chapter stands alone or is independent of the other chapters. Each chapter has valuable actions you can take now rather than waiting until you get to the end of the book. You can read only those chapters that seem relevant to the work you are doing today.

4. Non-sequential

You can read the chapters in whatever order makes sense to you. It is not necessary to start at the front of the book and read chapters in sequence. You can go straight to those chapters that appear to address your current concerns or situation.

5. Action-oriented

Action is an essential component of leadership. Each chapter will point toward action that matters in strategic execution, and will provide you with possible time frames for taking these actions.

6. Self-guided

Points of Inquiry are posted as an invitation for you to reflect on your current situation and consider actions that you could take. Also in several places, questions will be posted for you to assess yourself as a leader. These questions are tied to the content and you can use them as a reference if you see developmental opportunities for yourself.

7. **Addresses some of the peculiarities of human behavior**

   The Doors lead singer, Jim Morrison, used the haunting lyrics "People are strange" in the classic song of the same name. People are strange and get "stranger and stranger" during times of change. Leadership is the fine art of coalescing people with their peculiarities into a "collage of action that produces results". Too often those of us in management speak about change as if it were "paint by numbers", when in fact, each leadership challenge is unique and shaped by the odd collection of critters that are on the team or in the group.

   > *"People are strange…"*
   >
   > **Jim Morrison**

Is This the Right Book for You?

When I pick up a book I often start with the question "Is this the right book for me?" How can I know what this book is about and how practical will it be? In deciding if this is the right book for you, consider the following questions:

1. Are you currently involved in executing a strategy or contemplating becoming involved?
2. Are you concerned that the people component of the strategic execution be effectively led and managed?
3. Is the strategic execution predicated on extraordinary results being achieved?
4. Does your strategic execution constitute a large change for the business and organization?
5. Are you willing to consider unconventional approaches in order to enhance the magnitude of results?

If you answered yes to most of those questions, this book is for you.

This book is for you if you are:

- Involved
- Concerned that the people are led
- Extraordinary results
- Large change for the business
- Consider unconventional approaches

Let's get started! Grab a cup of coffee or tea, and let's begin our conversation.

Foundational Leaders

Preface

I am introducing you to a new term – "Foundational Leaders". Foundational Leaders is a term I have developed to communicate to you about the cornerstone of successful strategic execution. This cornerstone is authentic, real leadership. In business today we hear the term leaders and leadership tossed about in a wide variety of ways. In using the term Foundational Leader, I want to pull your attention to a particular type of leader who provides a particular type of leadership. This leadership is present when strategic execution is successful, and of course, is painfully missing when strategic execution fails.

Foundational Leaders are the cornerstone for successful execution. They are the center around which the direction of an execution project is based. Further, they build credibility for the organization and inspire others to act. Others being inspired and producing extraordinary results are the evidence of leadership. Inspiring others to act is also what is required for success in strategic execution. Yes, you need good strategies, well thought through implementation plans and modified processes, etc. Yet none of that matters if it is not implemented, and implementation invariably involves lots of people.

Strategic Execution

Achieving success in strategic execution is a daunting challenge for many businesses. Various authors say that half to two-thirds of execution projects fail to deliver the expected results. While there are a variety of explanations given, I say that the majority of reasons stem from lack of proper leadership. For most of you, you will immediately say "well of course". While it seems obvious, it is still so common. For more than twenty-five years I have been working along side of executives and managers in various forms of strategic executions. I have seen some stunning successes as well as, spectacular failures. I have seen certain executives be very successful in one setting only to fall short in the next setting. When I sit back and reflect on all these experiences, I keep coming back to the fundamental matter of leadership. That is Foundational Leadership for execution. Hence the title: *Foundational Leaders: Cornerstones of Successful Strategic Execution.*

Often I have heard the lament:

"This is the right thing to do and it is so easy *if only* they would do it"

If only is the key point in the sentence. "If only" is where "thinking about" confronts reality. Strategies and improved processes are only as good as the results produced. Results get produced when implemented. Implementation involves people. Usually lots of people. Further, many of those people will not immediately see any reason to be involved, much less to do something out of the ordinary.

In case you haven't noticed, telling people what to do seldom produces the desired effect. Sure you need to give them information, but information seldom inspires action. Leadership inspires action. Success in strategic execution begins with leaders. Authentic, real leaders earn the confidence, respect and trust of others, which of course is the opening for inspiring them to act.

This book, _Foundational Leaders: Cornerstones of Successful Strategic Execution_ focuses on these key leaders, and the being that they must bring to their work. This book deals with what the leaders need to have in place before stepping onto the field to provide leadership of strategic execution. The preparation and credibility of leaders is essential in strategic execution.

Disruption of Strategic Execution

Strategic execution requires dislodging of the status quo and implementation of substantive changes in how the business operates. For most of us, this level of change is not something we go into easily or feel excited about. On the contrary, we are usually dragged "kicking and screaming" into change. People look for assurance and confidence from significant others during change. Implementing a strategic change requires courage, skilled leaders and a series of well planned actions. Otherwise the intervention will hit too much resistance from the organization and will be abandoned or minimized. That is a common outcome, and the reason so many attempts at strategic execution fall short or are abandoned. Leadership is the first key ingredient for success in strategic execution.

Let's look at my definition of strategic execution:

> _Strategic execution is an intervention made into the trajectory of performance of a business. It is an interruption of the current trajectory in order to improve or upgrade the trajectory to one that will create more profitability and value in the business. Strategic execution is intentional actions designed to accomplish extraordinary results and position the business in a more attractive competitive position._

Strategic execution is an intervention made into the trajectory of performance of a business. It is an interruption of the current trajectory in order to improve or upgrade the trajectory to one that will create more profitability and value in the business. Interruption in the trajectory of a business's performance is neither something easily done nor an action to be taken lightly. It requires courage, skilled leaders and a series of well planned actions. Leadership is the first key ingredient for success in strategic execution.

Strategic execution is intended to create extraordinary results for the business. That is, prior to the interventions made in strategic execution neither the competitive position nor extraordinary results were possible. Strategic execution involves implementing discontinuous change and transformation, i.e., a change large enough to alter the form of the business, its performance and its position in its marketplaces. It is a substantive change that results in an appreciable difference in the competitiveness of the business. A strategic execution may or may not involve restructuring of the organization, but it should not, in any way be thought of as synonymous with organizational structure change. Rather it is a change in the fundamentals of the business, and will involve substantive changes in level of ownership and responsibility by employees. Additionally, you will see an increased velocity of actions, more engagement of people, greater speed at which decisions are made, more attention to the concerns of stakeholders, simplified work processes and burning passion for delivering results.

Importance of Leaders in Strategic Execution

I am often asked what makes strategic execution successful, and I reply "*leaders*". Usually there is a blank look back at me as if to say "Duh, well of course". It seems that often there is an assumption of a magic elixir that will assure execution success. Unfortunately the answer is nope, no magic pills. What is required is leaders doing what it takes to inspire their people to act in ways that will produce extraordinary results. This is probably common sense to you and something that you are well aware of. While it is common sense, it is so frequently NOT the case.

If success in execution being dependent of leadership is so straight forward, how come it is so often missed or not provided? Perhaps it is because there is a misunderstanding of what leaders do when implementing large scale changes like strategic execution and transformation. Let's look at nine points about leaders in strategic execution:

1. **There is confusion as to what constitutes leadership and who provides it.** Often I hear from others their expectation for what a leader should or should not be doing. While the person is well intended, their opinions are neither accurate nor useful. They have some internal picture of what a leader should do, how they should look, and what they should say that appear to be straight out of Hollywood casting. In reality, leaders of strategic execution are often front-line workers. They are the ones who know how to most dramatically change processes and improve performance. Other leaders are required to inspire them, but they are the ones who matter.

   How often do you hear the commentators in a sporting event describe the importance of the "unsung players"? In American football it is usually the line. The quality of the line often determines the outcome of the game even though "star" quarterbacks, receivers and running backs get all the attention. The game is won "in the trenches between the offensive and defensive lines". Likewise in strategic execution, the "game is won in the trenches".

How do you know leadership when you see it? I suggest that if you are looking at the top manager, you are probably starting at the wrong place. Begin by looking at those around the top manager. What do you see? I think leadership is best understood as the inspired actions of others producing extraordinary outcomes. Further, the inspired action of others produces more indigenous leaders in the trenches. The difference is made in the actions of others rather than in the actions of the "designated leader". Seems obvious, yes? Yet too often we pay too much attention to the "designated leader" or top manager and not nearly enough to the impact on others.

2. **Success in strategic execution requires focus on extraordinary performance.** Leaders call on others to challenge their ways of working and thinking, and to act in new ways. Challenging of current ways is part of the disruption and dislodging of the status quo. These new ways create extraordinary results.

   Strategic execution constitutes a major change for an organization. Change is best implemented when people actively participate and can see the impact of the extraordinary results for their business. Leadership inspires people not to settle for easy solutions, rather to look for extraordinary results and opportunities. Extraordinary results happen when people keep searching for actions to make their business "outrageously successful". Leadership is what drives teams to "settle only for the very best". Extraordinary outcomes are the intent of strategic execution and that occurs only due to leadership.

3. **Leadership is a relationship.** It starts with one person who commits to achieving a bold future for the business. The magnitude of this future will

speak to others in the business. While one person starts the conversation the actual leadership plays out in the interaction between multiple people. I have seen companies where the leadership of one person has a profound impact on thousands of employees, and in turn many more thousands of customers and shareholders. One leader can move many and create enormous value. What makes these leaders successful is the acceptance and actions of others.

4. **Leadership is personal and is based on personal relationships.**
   Leadership is a very dynamic process that is not readily amenable to mechanical approaches or rigid recipes. It is a creative process in which the leader searches and seeks out the right elements to inspire a group of people. Thus the work of the leader is never done. As long as one is leading, there must be a thirst for learning and improving ways to inspire others.

5. **Leadership is expansive and inclusive.** While the execution may begin with a limited number of leaders, if it is to be successful it is essential that leadership be provided at all levels of the organization. That is, the personal, relational aspects of leadership must be expanded to include many in the organization. The best leaders are often on the front-line. They are the ones who interface with customers and provide the products and services that make the business successful. They are also the ones that make the strategic execution successful. Therefore the success of the strategic execution is dependent on leadership provided by people who are not managers and not in positions of significant authority. The checkpoint is do you have leaders at all levels of the business?

6. **Leadership must be authentic.** If those who are expected to inspire others are not able and willing to be authentic, then they will be unsuccessful as a leader. That is, if a person is not committed and engaged in being personally involved, creating relationships and including others, they will be perceived as being inauthentic. That is, their actions will be perceived by others as being hollow. In fact I think the word tinny is a good description of how their behavior will be perceived by others. I like the word tinny as it describes a sound that is shallow and unpleasant. This is how employees experience an execution project when there is ineffective or insufficient leadership. Rather than being experienced as solid and attractive, there is an experience of inadequacy.

7. **Leadership is inseparable from communication.**
In philosophy there is the classic question of "what is the sound of one hand clapping"? I think a parallel is "what is the sound of a prospective leader talking to self"? Regardless of your answer to the one hand clapping question, I assert that leadership shows up in communication and relationship, not in isolation. There are particular kinds of communication and relationship that occur, which in turn inspire people's being and actions.

8. **Leaders have basic or foundational commitments that are the source of their leadership**. The check-point for an execution project is, will the leaders lead? Will there be the level and type of leadership provided that will make this execution as smooth as silk, or will it be as rough as a corn cob? Without appropriate leadership there is little chance that the execution will be successful. Leadership is the origin or source of successful execution. Without its source, the clarity, direction and momentum needed for success in execution simply will not be present.

9. **Leadership is the most critical component in all phases of strategic execution.** Certainly this is true of planning the strategic execution initiatives. Planning strategic execution is an expression of leadership. In business planning, we too often become enamored with the mechanical aspects of management, e.g., the six steps or the three really good tips to make something work. We attend to the mechanical aspects and miss the source that causes the success. Leadership is the cause of success in strategic execution. Leadership is not mechanical. There have been many attempts to make leadership mechanical, with predictable poor returns.

Foundational Leaders are the cornerstone for success in strategic execution. Like a cornerstone in building a wall, it takes just the right type of leaders to provide the proper foundation.

Importance of Leaders in Strategic Execution:

1. There is confusion as to what constitutes leadership and who provides it
2. Success in strategic execution requires extraordinary focus
3. Leadership requires a relationship
4. Leadership is personal and is based on personal relationships
5. Leadership is expansive and inclusive
6. Leadership is authentic
7. Leadership is inseparable from communication
8. Leaders must have foundational commitments that are the source of their leadership
9. Leadership is the most critical component in all phases of strategic execution

Foundational Leaders

1.

Foundational Leaders

Cornerstones of successful strategic execution

Introduction

There is overwhelming evidence that most strategic initiatives fall short of the expected results. At the core, these failures in execution are failures of leadership. These businesses have an organizational problem caused by lack of effective leadership. I assert that these leadership failures occur in part due to the lack of development and equipping of the prospective leaders in the foundations of leadership. Without proper foundations, these prospective leaders fail to establish credibility with their organization, fail to properly design the execution initiatives, fail to engage the various stakeholders, and are unable to inspire the people in the organization to act in an inspired manner. It all begins with solid foundations of leaders, or what in this writing I will call, "Foundational Leaders".

Foundational Leaders are often the rarest of elements in businesses. Too often there are few with the capability and credibility to provide genuine leadership.

Foundational Leaders

Instead those in management positions are more concerned with their own compensation and promotion and are unwilling to do anything that looks controversial or risky. Successful strategic execution is challenging, controversial and risky. It is not the domain of "yes people", but rather calls for authentic leaders.

Source of Foundational Leadership

Foundational leadership begins with the unique commitments of the person. I call these foundational commitments. These foundational commitments are developed over a lifetime and literally shape how the person sees their work, the business and the calling to be a leader. Chapter Two will present the origin and functioning of foundational commitments. In Chapter Three we will look at how foundational commitments provide the source for leaders in the midst of execution. Another way to think about source is the place from which one empowers and enables oneself to lead. In Chapter Four I will share with you how foundational commitments translate into leadership actions. The bottom line is that absent foundational commitments a person will not be an effective Foundational Leader and their positive impact on strategic execution will be minimal.

Upfront let me make a couple of points clear:
1. Deploying a person ***without*** foundational commitments into an execution leadership position is very risky. While these people may appear "popular" and may even achieve initial success, the long-term prognosis is very poor. These non-foundational leaders will invariably bring all the focus on themselves and miss all that is required to implement. Sooner or later you will find that these non-leaders have scudded the execution, or at least that you have no choice but to remove them from the role or at least build in much more complexity with a "work around".

2. Adults who do not have these foundational commitments are unlikely to gain them within a time frame of your project, if ever. If you think the non-leader is going to acquire foundational commitments and become a Foundational Leader, is a bit like the old saying of expecting a leopard to change its spots.

In stark contrast, people who are acting from their foundational commitments generally find clever and creative ways to make the execution successful. While there is always challenge and surprises, these Foundational Leaders have support of others in the organization that pulls for success even in challenging times.

While I opened this discussion speaking about managers, please understand that Foundational Leaders are needed at every level of the organization. Often some of the most impactful leadership comes from hourly employees who have commitment and passion for their business and are excellent at engaging and mobilizing others in the business.

Strategic Execution

Strategic Execution is an intervention made into the trajectory of the performance of a business. It is an interruption of the current trajectory in order to improve or upgrade the trajectory to one that will create more profitability and value in the business. Strategic Execution is intentional actions designed to accomplish extraordinary results and position the business in a more attractive competitive position.

> ***Strategic Execution is intended to create extraordinary results for the business.***

Foundational Leaders

Strategic Execution is intended to create extraordinary results for the business. That is, to achieve enhanced competitive position and business results. These outcomes do not happen by accident. Foundational Leaders make them happen. Foundational Leaders are the originating point for these interventions. Leaders guide others to design execution initiatives and then implement with energy, intensity and integrity.

> *Strategic execution involves implementing discontinuous change and transformation, i.e., a change large enough to alter the form of the business, its performance and its position in its marketplaces.*

It is a substantive change that results in an appreciable difference in the competitiveness of the business. A Strategic Execution may or may not involve restructuring of the organization, but it should not in any way be thought of as synonymous with organizational structure change. Rather it is change in the fundamentals of the business, and will involve substantive changes in level of ownership and responsibility by employees, engagement of people, increased velocity of actions, speed at which decisions are made, attention to the concerns of stakeholders, simplified work processes and burning passion for delivering results. All of these things occur through the influence and impact of Foundational Leaders.

Strategic execution planning begins with the leaders articulating the business case for the change. This leadership message of the business case needs to be compelling for all those who will be involved in planning and implementing the initiative, as well as, those who will be impacted by the change. Too often the business case is not well articulated and/or does not contain anything "compelling" for stakeholders. Too often managers describe some ethereal benefit that has nothing to do with employees, and then are shocked when their people do not get "on-board" for the change. Often the believability of the business case is as much from the speaker as the message itself. The speaker must speak from the heart and clearly articulate personal commitment to the success of the initiative. Absent the clarity of leadership commitment, the business case will likely have little power to engage people's interest and enroll them in taking actions required for success.

Foundational leadership must also be provided in elevating the level of thinking during planning, as well as throughout all of the execution. That is, a "dab of leadership" at the kickoff of the Execution effort is not sufficient. Leadership must be provided over time and in the trenches during the challenging days of planning and implementation. Execution is more than a role of leadership. It is the essence of leadership.

Examples of Lack of Foundational Leaders

Foundational Leaders have learned over time that execution requires intense preparation, rigorous logistics and passionate implementation. You will see that many initiatives fall short because of the lack of anticipation of what it will actually take to make it work and the impact it will have on employees and other key stakeholders. Too often there are naïve managers who mean well, but are clueless as to what will be required for success. Some of these managers think, "Just tell 'em what to do and get on with it". While this sounds "strong" in meetings, it is actually a dangerous blend of arrogance, bravado and naivety. In addition to alienating employees, this approach very rarely delivers the expected results and is almost certainly never sustained. Other managers are optimistically hoping that everyone will welcome the change brought about by the initiatives.

What these managers misunderstand is what they are getting into. Strategic Execution is an intervention made into the trajectory of performance of a business. It is an interruption of the current trajectory in order to improve or upgrade the trajectory to one that will create more profitability and value in the business. Interruption in the trajectory of a business's performance is neither something easily done nor an action to be taken lightly. It requires courage, skilled leaders and a series of well planned actions. This includes:

1. Foundational Leaders setting the context for execution that is solid and appreciated by all those who will be involved in implementation.
2. Foundational Leaders appreciate the importance of gaining a broad cross section of ideas and input in planning phases.
3. Foundational Leaders appreciate the challenges involved in actually implementing the initiative and planning accordingly.
4. Foundational Leaders guide others in designing the initiatives FROM implementation. Understanding what can be successfully implemented is the key to developing strategy and initiatives.
5. Foundational Leaders actively engage the various stakeholders in the planning phase to assure the initiative was understood and if unforeseen problems existed to discover these problems prior to launching implementation. If stakeholders are not engaged prior to launch there is good chance they will be covertly to overtly resistive to the changes being brought about by the initiative.

Foundational Leaders are essential in each step of execution. They cannot show up occasionally. Rather they must be intimately involved throughout. Otherwise the intervention will hit too much resistance from the organization and will be abandoned or minimized. That is a common occurrence, and the reason so many attempts at strategic execution fall short or abandoned.

We are great at developing strategies and plans…
but lousy at implementing.

How often have you heard this lament? How often do we come up with good ideas and then see these ideas shrivel because of poor implementation? We lament this situation not only because we see the lost opportunity but also because we feel a kind of resignation that anything can really be done to change the way things are done in the business.

The inability to implement effectively is what leads to low-quality products, obsolete technology, poor customer service, weak sales, poor returns on capital projects, failure to control operating costs…all the things that are described as the cause of shareholder value destruction. A manager once gave a great description of this when he said, "In our business, we have a lot of takeoffs but very few landings."

This is a metaphor for starting many change initiatives but seeing most of them disappear and never be completed. Imagine an actual airport where you could see takeoffs and also see the landscape littered with the wreckage of prior "project flights." Such a scene would not encourage flights. Past failed initiatives, likewise, do not encourage people to be excited about new initiatives.

Attempts at Strategic Execution absent Foundational Leaders

Countless studies have found that a majority of strategic executions fail to deliver the expected results. For example, in a 2006 McKinsey Quarterly online survey[1], only 38% of the global executives who responded said that their recent transformations had been "completely" or "mostly" successful in impacting performance. About 10% rated their transformation efforts as "completely" or "mostly" unsuccessful.

In their classic book, *Execution: The Discipline of Getting Things Done*, Larry Bossidy and Ron Charan [2]assert that there are three key points to remember:
1. Execution is a discipline and integral to strategy.
2. Execution is the major role of the business leader.
3. Execution must be a core element of an organization's culture.

While I strongly agree with these points, I think it is important to add Foundational Leadership at all levels of the business. My core message is that leadership is the cornerstone for success in Strategic Execution. I learned a wonderful expression called *full stop* from a British client. When a speaker reaches the end of a point or has spoken the essence of the communication, the speaker will say *full stop*. It means that what needed to be said has been said clearly and there is nothing else to say about that. There is no need to try and refine the point, as what has been said, is as well said as the speaker can make it. (And of course we all have had the experience of continuing to talk after the point has been made and finding that we "muddy up" clarity on the subject). Given that

---

[1] *Organizing for Successful Change Management: A McKinsey Global Survey*. The McKinsey Quarterly. July 2006

[2] Larry Bossidy and Ram Charan. *Execution: The Discipline of Getting Things Done*. Crown Business. New York, New York, 2002

Foundational Leaders

background explanation, please hear this statement: "The foundation for successful strategic execution is intentional, foundational leadership...*full stop*."

Please hear that I am saying Foundational Leaders must be at all levels of your organization if it is to be successful in strategic execution. Too often I say leaders and people hear me as saying executives. Of course having executives be effective Foundational Leaders is very important. Yet executives can actually do very little by themselves. Rather, an executive's role as a leader is to create other leaders throughout the business and in particular to aid in planning and acting to make the strategic execution successful. Too often there is too much attention paid to the executive leaders. Yes they are the starting point, and yet successful execution does not occur without effective leadership at all levels of the organization. Said another way, the tendency is to pay too much attention to executive leaders and too little to hourly leaders.

Actions of Foundational Leaders

- **Create a future**
- **Commit to outcomes (specific banner results)**
- **Provide clear direction and design for implementation**
- **Engage the right people**
- **Exhibit persistence and tenacity**

A cadre of Foundational Leaders is mandatory for success in strategic execution and transformation. Foundational Leaders are capable of and committed to producing extraordinary results in the business. A Foundational Leader is determined and responsible. The leader is willing to be responsible for raising the level of conversations during the planning phase. That is, asking questions, challenging the level of analysis and thinking, calling into question when the thinking is inward or isolated, refusing to accept easy answers, and continuing to push for thinking that will lead to extraordinary results. During the planning phase the leaders make it explicit that they expect others to take actions in areas that are beyond their formal accountability as part of the strong commitment to seeing the business produce exceptional results and succeed. Creating extraordinary results usually involves working across organizational borders and boundaries, so it is important that leadership establishes the intention to collaborate and work across traditional organizational boundaries during the planning phase of execution. Let's now look at some of the actions of Foundational Leaders.

Create a New Future
Successful strategic execution begins in the future. One role of the Foundational Leader is to create and communicate a compelling future for the business. This future is more compelling and rewarding than what is predicted given current performance. This future will be of value to a variety of stakeholders including employees and owners. Foundational Leaders create effective strategic execution initiatives from the outcomes in the future that will assure success of the business.

While this may seem odd at first, it is essential for success in strategic execution. I am amazed at how odd this feels for many managers since we think from the future in many aspects of our lives. Yet when it comes to implementing initiatives most of us have not learned to think this way. Let me give you an analogy. If you needed to be in New York City tomorrow for a meeting, what would you do? You would think about the starting time of the meeting, and work back to develop your travel arrangements. For most of you that is an act that you do with little regard for what has happened to you in the past, unless of course you had a bad experience on a recent flight with a particular airline or previously you have a bad experience with a hotel in New York. Bad memories aside, you start with a future you wish to create (on time for my meeting, arrive fresh and well rested) and plan back from that. In a subsequent chapter we will discuss planning from the future in much more detail. For now let's say that it is an essential element of leadership in strategic execution.

Committing to Specific Outcomes

Another element of Foundational Leadership is identifying outcomes that are to be achieved by the strategic execution. These outcomes need to be sufficiently large that it will alter the competitive position of the business, and produce substantive value creation. Often there is reticence to identity outcomes this large, since the leader does not know how it can be achieved. That is precisely the point of courage for leadership. It is committing to achieving an outcome without being able to show all the steps required to successfully deliver the result. Often the leader can agree to this level of outcomes since competitors are already accomplishing similar results, and the task at hand is to build on what competitors are doing and advance beyond.

Confronting Reality & Challenging Organizational Myths

The leader's impact also shows up as challenging the myths that may have developed about the business, organization and the products of the business. As a sequel to _Execution_, Bossidy and Charan wrote _Confronting Reality_. In this book they noted that too often Executions fail because the executives and managers failed to confront the reality of their situation. A leader must show openness to inquiry and challenge even the most sensitive topics. The leader must be explicit if an area is "off limits", and then declare everything else open to investigation and questioning. Employees assume there are many more "sacred cows", or topics off limits, than is usually the case. Establishing clarity on what is available for inquiry is a key first step in confronting reality. A second key step is to insist on facts rather than opinions and interpretations. The leader's role is to bring crispness and thoroughness to thinking, without locking in on "our tired old answers".

Clarity of Direction and Design

A classic question employees have is, "Where are we going, and how are we going to get there"? Leadership is demonstrated in providing clear crisp answers to these questions. Direction is explicit in terms of the future we are going after as well as the outcomes that will demonstrate our success in reaching this future. How we are going to get there is demonstrated through an architecture or design for the full execution, including the core initiatives. These initiatives are developed from a point in the future back to the present. The architecture gives clarity and meaning to the initiatives, and demonstrates that if executed properly the strategic initiatives will produce tremendous results for the business. Once the initiatives are seen as viable, the next question is involving the right people in preparing for implementation.

Engaging the Right People

Getting the right people involved is essential. For people in the organization the evidence of how serious the leaders are about the execution project is demonstrated by who is engaged to be part of the projects. If the leaders are willing to ask the tough questions, an air of credibility is established. If on the other hand, those involved are "the usual suspects", it is a clear signal to those in the organization that nothing has changed nor will change. The selection of team leaders and team members is among the strongest communications that the leadership can give stakeholders about how strongly committed they are to the success of the execution and initiatives.

Persistence and Tenacity

Leaders also appreciate that their job is never done while in the midst of strategic execution. A transformational leader appreciates that they are the source of action in the business. If the actions of the organization are off trajectory or missing the target, the leader does not jump to blaming employees. Rather the leader looks to see what he/she has missed or not provided. The leader sees self as source of the actions of others. This provides the leader with much greater access to altering the behaviors of employees.

Leadership Intention

Strategic Execution requires intentionality. That is, a leader being intentional about achieving the results. This brings clarity and focus on what is required for success. They are focused on accomplishing the task at hand. Many executives are unaware of the demands that Strategic Execution will place on them. In particular, there is a demand to be an intentional leader. This not only includes ways of being and acting on the executive's part but also that executive's ability to inspire employees throughout the business also to be leaders. Discontinuous or transformational leadership actually calls for leaders to emerge at all levels of the organization.

Uniqueness of Foundational Leaders

Foundational Leadership should not be taken for granted. In most businesses there are not as many Foundational Leaders as you would like. Hence the challenge

A Foundational Leader assures a thirst for learning and expanding the capability of self and others to lead.

facing leaders is to engage others who have the proper foundational commitments to emerge as Foundational Leaders. Often you will find these people in unusual places, e.g., a supervisor, a quiet staff person, in the union hall. Often you will NOT find them in the places that you would hope, e.g., direct reports, management teams or human resources.

In addition to their being a predictable shortage of Foundational Leaders, there is also the challenge that there is not a "quick recipe for success". Each strategic execution and transformation is different. Each has unique challenges. A Foundational Leader must be open to learning, wiling to taste bitter failure while in the midst of winning the war, be thrilled by the success of others and willing to be bigger than the circumstances. This person is quite serious about being and doing what is required to see that the employees in the organization are successful in bringing about the transformation. Absent leadership, attempted intervention into the trajectory of the business will fail and the results will not be achieved.

A Foundational Leader assures a thirst for learning and expanding the capability of self and others to lead. This leadership is demonstrated in planning as well as actions taken in the midst of execution. There is an old military quote that is applicable to strategic execution. "Only a fool goes into execution of a strategy without a plan, and only a fool refuses to modify and upgrade the plan once execution begins." It could be said that strategic execution is acting to implement a thorough and thoughtful plan.

Successful execution requires having hourly employees and supervisors as Foundational Leaders.

Successful execution requires having hourly employees and supervisors as Foundational Leaders. These front-line leaders will ultimately determine the success of the execution. Let's use an analogy from the military. Strategic Execution is the arena in which officers and soldiers in the field implement the strategy that was created by the Generals. Even with the best of design and planning, the implementation will encounter unforeseen problems once in implementation that have to be solved "in the field or on the ground." This means that there must be leadership at the top and there must be leadership among all employees in order to invent solutions to new and unprecedented problems. No General today plans a campaign and then goes on to other tasks. The General stays engaged in leading the campaign and inspires the women and men carrying out the General's plan to be leaders in the day-to-day implementing of the General's campaign plan. This same kind of leadership is what is required of those who plan the strategy for a discontinuous change if victory is to be achieved. Just as "no battle plan ever won a battle," so no strategy is valid until it is executed. The skills that are required to implement a strategy are what make business exciting and rewarding. The heroism of employees in finding ways to make things happen is what carries the day. All of this occurs because of the intentional type of leadership that is provided by executives that makes it safe for employees to step up and contribute, i.e., to be leaders themselves.

Most managers are interested in being thought of as a leader, yet a much smaller number are willing to do what it takes to *be* a leader. That is, many managers lack the capability and willingness to act in ways that create disruption in the business and inspire employees as needed to successfully execute the strategies. Foundational Leadership is demonstrated in Strategic Execution, and pretenders or pseudo-leaders are revealed.

Becoming a Foundational Leader

At this point I would like to turn the conversation and speak directly to you, as if we were sitting in your work space talking about this subject of you being a foundational leader. At this point it should be clear that I say foundational leaders are the cornerstone of successful strategic execution. Yet that does not make it so. It takes people like you to make it happen. So at this point you would likely ask me, "OK, where do I start". My answer is short and to the point. You begin with yourself. If you are going to be a successful foundational leader, you must begin with yourself. In the next three chapters we will look at commitments. These are the commitments that share you as well as those you choose to have around you. It is predictable that you will discover that you will benefit from making your commitments more public and visible to those around you. This will be a change for you.

If you as a leader are unwilling to change, there is no reason to expect others in the organization to follow. Gandhi sums this up well:

> ### *"To change, first we must change ourselves"*
> **Gandhi**

You lead through communication, examples and your openness to deal with surprises and unexpected events. You must be willing to make personal changes as required for the success of the business. That is, you as a leader must be aware that you will need to go first in making personal changes and process changes.

Conclusion

Success in strategic execution occurs as a consequence of Foundational Leaders. Foundational Leaders assure there is good strategic thinking, designing of a do-able plan, engaging employees at all levels of the organization, and tenaciously sorting through the interruptions and surprises until the results are achieved. It begins and ends with leadership. No leader, no success in strategic execution.

Foundational Leaders

Summary Points:

1. Foundational leaders set the context for execution
2. Foundational leaders appreciate the importance of gaining a broad cross section of ideas and input in the planning phase
3. Foundational leaders appreciate the challenges involved in actually implementing the initiative and planning accordingly
4. Foundational leaders guide others in designing the initiatives FROM implementation.
5. Foundational leaders actively engage the various stakeholders in the planning phase to assure the initiative was understood and if unforeseen problems existed to discover these problems prior to launching implementation.

Foundational Leaders

2.

Foundational Commitments

A key to leadership in strategic execution

Foundational leadership must be present for highly successful strategic execution to be achieved. This kind of leadership is required since most strategic execution projects are a departure from business as usual. Successful execution involves achievement of extraordinary results in business performance and value creation. Foundational leadership is not given by position, by authority, or by delegation. Foundational leadership does not happen by accident. Rather, effective leadership is caused by the leader. Foundational leadership is created or generated on a day-to-day basis by the leader for the specific purpose of achieving extraordinary results in business performance and value creation. Foundational commitments are the bedrock source for an individual being able to generate leadership.

Foundational Leaders

The Ground of Foundational Commitments

The root word of *foundational* is "to found". We all know what it means to found something. People found colleges, their children's investment funds, and companies. To found is to establish something on a solid basis. If we trace the word found back to its origins, we finally get to the ancient Latin word for "bottom". When something is founded, it rests on a very bottom tenet, principle or stand.

> *"Knowing yourself is the beginning of wisdom."*
> **Aristotle**

Leaders who are effective in bringing about extraordinary business results and value creation found their leadership on bedrock principles from which no circumstance can shake them. These leaders who operate from foundational commitments invent conversations and behaviors based on never-changing tenets that reflect the very ground of being that sources what the leaders stand for. Leaders sourced by their own foundational commitments then enact the conversations they have invented. These actions and conversations come from the base - the bottom - of what the leader believes makes life and work worthwhile and meaningful.

A metaphor for foundational commitments is the cornerstone in a building. The cornerstone is the first step in building the foundation of a building and the critical support on which everything else is built. Likewise, the foundational commitments of a leader are the fundamentals from which individuals create their being.

Foundational Leaders

This creation process occurs moment to moment throughout the day. That is, leaders give themselves over to these foundational commitments as a ground of being. The foundational commitments create the context in which leaders think and work. The leaders operate from foundational commitments rather than from opinions, concerns and worries. Given this ground of being, leaders are able to see what is needed to forward the work of a team or the business and invent the actions and conversations that will produce the intended consequences.

Foundational Commitments Matter

The first invented conversation foundational commitment leaders have with themselves is "thinking", and it is what provides the leaders with a clear perspective on the situation. The behaviors and conversations that result from this thinking provide the energy and possibility for others to understand the action that is being requested. In addition, the conversations that are sourced by the leader's foundational commitments provide the employees with the opportunity to assess the leader to determine if they can trust this person and want to risk becoming involved in the action being requested.

Leaders must operate from foundational commitments in order to establish credibility with the people in the organization. If the people have the sense that the leader is the "real deal," there is appreciation for what is said, even if it is hard to hear. There is the sense that the leader is being honest, candid and speaking from the heart.

Most individuals in a company say they espouse some form of beliefs and values. The question is: are these beliefs and values expedient and in-the-moment or are these beliefs and values stable and authentic?

Foundational Leaders

> *The beliefs and values of a leader who operates from foundational commitments are stable and authentic.*

The beliefs and values of a leader who operates from foundational commitments are stable and authentic. They are actively demonstrated and readily expressed. They are practiced in everyday life. These beliefs and values shape the being of the leader, which, in turn, forms the basis for personal motivation and perspective. Personal motivation and perspective, in turn, become the foundation for the actions that the leader takes. Foundational commitments live as consistent core actions and conversations and, because the commitments are authentic, the leader is able to enroll others to do the hard work of achieving extraordinary performance.

Examples of Foundational Commitments

- **Integrity**
- **Candor**
- **Learning**
- **Inspiring the actions of others**
- **Motives for change clear and above question**
- **Value creation**.
- **Well-being of the people**
- **Development of the capability of the organization**
- **Boldness**
- **Continual striving to improve performance regardless of current success**
- **Sharing the rewards with those who helped achieve them**

Foundational Leaders

While foundational commitments are unique for each individual, there is a common set that I have seen present in the successful leaders with whom I have been privileged to work. These include:

- **Integrity**. A commitment to speak the truth and to be known as a member of that group of human beings who do what they say they will do and whose word is their "bond."
- **Candor**. A willingness to be complete and to speak directly in conversations, i.e., appreciation for "straight talk."
- **Learning**. An exhibited thirst for continual learning and knowledge.
- **Inspiring the actions of others**. A desire to walk the talk and also a desire to see others walking the talk.
- **Motives for change clear and above question**. A strong desire for the motives for change to be experienced as authentic and in the best interest of the whole. Also, a strong desire not to be seen as self-serving or taking actions for personal benefit.
- **Value Creation**. A commitment to creating value for the stakeholders of the operation and company first, with less attention to what is in one's personal best interest.
- **Well-being of the people**. A passion for the safety and well-being of the employees and customers. Safety becomes a guiding light.
- **Development of the capability of the organization**. Candor about the organization's current capabilities to execute the strategy. This translates into intense focus on what is needed for development of the functional capabilities of the organization. Also, there is commitment to development of employees as individuals.
- **Boldness**. A willingness to be bold if not outrageous at times in order to lead the organization to achieve the needed results.

- **Continual striving to improve performance regardless of current success**. An unwillingness to settle for second best. A practice of looking forward to the next opportunity or challenge. A practice of not allowing complacency or arrogance to settle in.
- **Sharing the rewards with those who helped achieve them**. A clear plan for recognizing, acknowledging and rewarding those individuals in the company who helped create the success.

Foundational Commitments in Action

It is not hard to identify the foundational commitments of this sailing team leader as he writes about a recent race:

> *Day #5 – Final Day* - *A fun, yet hard fought day. Today's single race was the "Medal Race" for the Regatta. Ten boats, one race, places count double on a very short course. Very exciting. Press boats and coaches swarmed the course area. Multi classes all starting on the same course at varied start times.*
>
> *The breeze was mid-teens with some higher and lower gusts. We had a good start mid-line. Some boats piled up on the pin end. We stayed on Starboard with the Brits, took a tack to the right but didn't get far enough right as the far right came in. We rounded the top mark about mid fleet. Racing was close! No spinnaker as the reach was too tight. No boat set. We set at the reach mark and only gibed once to the leeward. It was a very short leg!! We tried to catch a shift on the next beat and were somewhat successful; however, the beat was already over by the time we got into the shift. We rounded one gibe, rounded the leeward mark as the Italians capsized in front of us, held off the Israelis at the finish, and took*

6th. An okay result in a tough fleet. It surely could have been better. The race was over before we knew it! Lessons learned: This was our first experience with the new format. We need to get used to this new format, particularly on such a short course in a breeze. It is fun, no doubt about it.

We remain very excited by our performance this week. Moreover, we've become more comfortable in some conditions we previously had speed problems with. Mid-teens velocities are now becoming a strong suit. We keep upping our top wind velocity comfort levels. We have much to do, but we like the trajectory and wind velocity comfort levels.

If we wanted to abstract from this communication the foundational commitments of the leader of this sailing team, we might list phrases like these: *commitment to winning; commitment to learning; commitment to making positive use of setbacks and failures; commitment to seeing situations as they are and telling the truth about these situations to the best of the leader's ability.*

Business leaders who achieve extraordinary results and create value, just like sports professionals, act from commitments which are bedrock. While these foundational commitments may not be so easy to identify and articulate in the business world as in the sport of sailing, they nevertheless inform that everything the leader does just as fully as do the commitments of the head of this sailing team. It is a most worthwhile activity, therefore, for a business leader to examine what foundational commitments create his or her conversations and actions so that these conversations and actions become conscious and can be articulated to everyone in the organization.

Foundational Commitments Are Not Synonymous with Company Values Statements

While I encourage businesses to have dialogs with employees about shared values and how those values relate to the future of the business, this kind of dialog is not what I am referencing when I talk about foundational commitments. Unfortunately, too often the development of "value statements" has been an exercise or a fashionable thing for management to do. For the past few decades, consultants and management gurus have encouraged business teams to develop such value statements. Rarely, in fact, do I encounter a business that does not have a value statement. When surveyed, employees will tell you that the company does have a values statement and that it is hanging on the wall in the lobby, the lunchroom and/or the copy room. When asked, however, if that values statement is practiced or experienced as "real," the employees say that the values statement has made little difference in the running of the company.

The gap between what the management team says is the value of the company and the actual practices becomes a significant challenge for the leader who is committed to achieving extraordinary results. This gap can be closed only when leaders act every day from foundational commitments that stand solid. It is only such authentic invented conversations and actions that can ever give any meaning to the company's values statements.

Foundational Commitments: Not Everyone Has "Got 'Em":

Not everyone who has jobs of responsibility in an organization acts from foundational commitments. In some companies, it is rare to find managers who are willing to step up and lead from foundational commitments. For a variety of reasons, many managers operate from pseudo-commitment. Rather than coming from foundational commitments, a pseudo-commitments driven manager looks to the political environment of the organization for guidance. That is, this person looks for clues of the behavior that will win acceptance and approval by others in the organization. The pseudo-commitment manager's behavior is designed to gain acceptance, approval and praise from others, not necessarily to produce business results.

Pseudo-commitments lead to behaviors and conversations based on (1) what these individuals think will make them good impression, (2) what they think will please their superiors, or (3) what they think is the expedient thing to do at the moment. The mantra of the pseudo-commitment manager is, "Tell me what to do, and I will go do it."

A good way to think of pseudo-commitments is to consider situational ethics. In situational ethics, no action is wrong in and of itself; it is, rather, the situation in which the action occurs that determines whether an action is good or bad. Situational ethics change with the circumstances. What is wrong or right - or what I believe or don't believe - is shaped by the circumstances or surroundings. When in Rome, do as Romans do.

Managers who operate from pseudo-commitments are like individuals who live by situational ethics. These managers are a significant liability to the leader who is working from foundational commitments to achieve extraordinary results. This is because individuals who live by pseudo-commitments are often very good at jumping on the bandwagon of the next program or process that comes along because they think it is politically correct to do so. These individuals will involve themselves in a current program and appear to be doing and saying the right things, even when they are actually not doing what is expected.

Pseudo-commitment managers may be hard to spot early on, because they are usually excellent at "managing up." They say all the right things and appear to be carrying out the intent of the people to whom they report. Over time however, telltale signs expose these pseudo-commitment managers so that it becomes clear they are not actually doing what is expected of them.

Pseudo-commitment managers may be hard to spot early on, because they are usually excellent at "managing up." They say all the right things and appear to be carrying out the intent of the people to whom they report.

The evidence that an individual is operating from pseudo-commitments rather than from foundational commitments is the results accomplished in something other than business as usual. For example, look at projects and responses to challenges. Examine how many initiatives this individual has started and how few have actually been completed and produced results. People around this kind of manager will say things like, "We've had a lot of takeoffs, but very few landings." Most of these initiatives simply disappeared during the night. At first, this evidence appears as "accidents," or a time-specific explainable event. Then a pattern starts to develop.

The danger that these pseudo-commitment managers pose to genuine foundational commitment leaders is that they poison the organization to the possibility of excellent performance and extraordinary result.

The danger that these pseudo-commitment managers pose to genuine foundational commitment leaders is that they poison the organization to the possibility of excellent performance. Pseudo-commitment manager's agreements quickly dissipate when they are faced with making difficult decisions and taking unpopular actions. A classic example is of a pseudo-commitments manager who is unwilling to confront a direct report who is an "ally," even though this employee is clearly "misbehaving." This misbehavior can show up as not taking agreed upon actions, not producing the expected results or not following the agreed-upon strategy. The pseudo-commitment manager will find many reasons and excuses not to take needed action with the "ally." Rather than confronting what needs to be dealt with, the pseudo-commitment managers will ignore the problem, head off in another direction, or stall until the momentum of the program dissipates. This behavior results in others in the organization becoming quite aware of the inauthentic nature of the manager's commitment. This awareness leads to a fundamental lack of trust for that person.

> *A pseudo-commitment manager can do much to undermine the credibility of the foundational-commitment leader and the effort to achieve extraordinary result performance. Pseudo-commitment managers behave in ways that are quite inconsistent with the commitment and intent of the foundational leader, even though it may not be apparent at first.*

While this behavior may be hidden from the leader, it is not hidden from the people in the organization. If the leader who wants to achieve extraordinary performance actually uses the pseudo-commitments manager, the people assume that neither of them is serious about the performance improvement and ignore the change efforts.

What separates these two types of commitments: foundational and pseudo-commitments? Foundational commitments are internally generated and are not derived from the situation alone but are reflective of the individual's deepest commitments. By contrast, pseudo-commitments are superficial and serve the agenda of the individual. Pseudo-commitments also result in unproductive behaviors that employees can identify in a heartbeat.

Examples of Pseudo Commitments

- **Situational ethics rather, than integrity in action and speech**
- **Dissembling rather, than candor**
- **Short-term actions, rather than long-term actions**
- **Well being of supporters, rather than well being of all the employees**
- **Adhering to a personal perspective, rather than being open to examine the unknown and the more difficult**
- **Being popular and well-regarded are more important than winning**
- **Complacency, rather than continual striving to improve performance.**
- **Support for the correctness of approach, rather than learning**
- **Goal of compliance of others, rather than inspired actions of others**
- **Looking out for # 1 (Self)**

When asked to describe the characteristics of an individual who operates with pseudo-commitments, employees identify behaviors like these:

- **Situational ethics rather than integrity in action and speech.** The person is driven by the need to get approval and make a good impression with other managers.

- **Dissembling rather than candor.** This person is candid only so long as this candor does not reflect negatively on their supporters or themselves. They may become agitated at the request for "straight talk."
- **Short-term actions rather than long-term actions**. The pseudo-commitments individual focuses on what seems useful to do today rather than taking on the harder, long-term actions that create value.
- **Well being of supporters, rather than well being of all the employees.** This individual does not have a commitment to all, but looks after her or his "own."
- **Adhering to a personal perspective rather than being open to examine the unknown and the more difficult.** These individuals who operate from pseudo-commitments will surround themselves with "loyalists" who agree with their personal perspectives. These pseudo-commitment managers are unwilling to question their perspective, to venture into the unknown, or to make difficult or unpopular decisions.
- **Being popular and well-regarded are more important than winning.** This person is always looking for approval and chooses popularity over making a tough call.
- **Complacency rather than continual striving to improve performance.** This person will not address underperforming employees if these people are their supporters. Nor will this person be aggressive in dealing with problems with customers.
- **Support for the correctness of approach rather than learning.** The pseudo-commitment manager focuses on rules and procedures rather than being willing to accept the messiness that is inherent in learning new ways to operate in order to achieve extraordinary results.
- **Goal of compliance of others rather than inspired actions of others.** The individuals who operate from pseudo-commitments will not give leeway for people who work for them to create new ways of working that inspire others;

instead, they focus on having individuals be compliant and follow the old ways of operation.

- **Looking out for # 1 (Self) and doing what's self-serving, rather than sharing the rewards with others.** These individuals are not interested in others being recognized and rewarded if this means that less attention and rewards will be forthcoming for themselves.

The characteristics are not hard to spot, especially by front-line employees. They mark conversations and actions that cannot produce extraordinary results or create value.

From the Mouths of Children

There is a children's book that captures the behaviors of pseudo-commitment managers in an amusing and enlightening way. _Me Too Iguana_ by Jacquelyn Reinach and Richard Hefter[3] is the story of an iguana that gets herself into trouble by trying to become like every animal she runs into and then forgets who and what she really is. Whatever animal the little iguana sees, she wants to be, rather than be herself.

> When the iguana sees an elephant in the grocery store, she goes home and gets a rubber hose, paints it gray, and ties it to her nose so that she can be an elephant. When she sees a lion in the barbershop, she goes home and puts yellow wool all over her head so that people will think she is a lion. When she saw a stork fly over the post office, the iguana set off home to make wings so she could fly. At every turn, the iguana tries to hide her true identity so that she will look like other types of animals.

---

[3] Jacquelyn Reinach, Richard Hefter (Illustrator). _Me Too Iguana_ (_Sweet Pickles Series_). Henry Holth & Co. March 1977.

While this is a cute story for children, it is, unfortunately, also a description of the pseudo-commitment managers. One of my colleagues had the occasion to work for a master pseudo-commitment manager. My colleague's wife could, early on, see the pseudo-commitments behavior of the manager and began to refer to her husband's boss as "the iguana," based on the main character in this children's book. I have told this story a number of times, and each time the listeners quickly identify the iguanas in their own work experience.

Separating the Goats from the Sheep

Leaders who live by foundational commitments are keenly aware of the liability posed by pseudo-commitment managers. Even when these pseudo-commitment managers are saying the right thing and appearing enthusiastic, the leader with authentic foundational commitments will, over time, begin to see the wrong behaviors that come from the thinness of the person's commitments.

The challenge in strategic execution is creating extraordinary business results and value creation. This calls on the leaders to identify quickly those individuals who are driven by pseudo-commitments. If a manager is driven by pseudo-commitments, it is unlikely that he or she will be successful in leading any change needed to create extraordinary results or increase value. Absent the foundational commitments that ring true, the individual simply will not have the courage to take "tough positions," to have difficult conversations with "allies," nor enough credibility with the employees to motivate them to take the actions needed to get the results. Employees are usually keenly aware of which of their supervisors and managers are shaped by pseudo-commitments and which are shaped by foundational commitments. In fact, many employees have seen previous change efforts falter and fail because of the behavior of pseudo-commitment managers and are skeptical of all leaders, imagining that every leader works this way.

What the leader who is driving toward excellent performance must appreciate is that the managers currently in place were successful in an old culture. They found ways to adapt and thrive in that culture. If not, they would not be in their current positions.

If the goals for improvement in performance require significant contextual and cultural change, then these current managers must also significantly change. The critical

> *What the leader who is driving extraordinary results in performance must appreciate is that the managers currently in place were successful in an old culture.*

question is what will be the cause or source of the change: pseudo-commitments or foundational commitments? If people change simply to please the new boss, it will not work out. The current managers must find the motivation for change from within and this motivation must be based on a solid *bottom* of foundational commitments.

Often finding the motivation for change from within is very difficult for people who have become successful by being "popular" and "politically correct." Those who thrived in the old culture may be the last ones to make the change, given that they are the best at being what was expected and rewarded in the old culture. This is a crucial point in strategic execution. While the people may have long tenure with the company, extensive industry experience and great academic credentials, they may not be able to make such a fundamental shift.

> *Individuals' ability to be grounded in foundational commitments is a primary determinant of whether these people will make the necessary changes. Hence, it is important to determine who has clear foundational commitments that will work in the new culture and strategy.*

Foundational Leaders

Individuals' ability to be grounded in foundational commitments is a primary determinant of whether these people will make the necessary changes. Hence, it is important to determine who has clear foundational commitments that will work in the new culture and strategy. This determination is very crucial in strategic execution where there has to be significant organizational change in order to achieve improved performance.

Conclusion

Foundational commitments are bedrock stands that *are* who a leader is. These foundational commitments become invented conversations leaders hold with themselves and with those around them. Foundational commitments are a demonstration of leadership since they provide the energy and possibility for others to discover foundational commitments for themselves and, ultimately, to generate their own unique expressions of foundational-commitment leadership. The invention of foundational commitments provides an opening for thinking and action by others.

Foundational commitments are the source of leadership. They are what give energy, direction and guidance to the leader who is in the midst of implementing significant change in order to achieve extraordinary results and value creation. Foundational commitments are what give authenticity and candor to the speaking of the leader and what makes the communication about the need for change land well with the employees. It is important that there is "obviousness" to the leader's behavior and conversations. It should be clear that the desired results will benefit the business and the location and will provide some benefit or gain for the employees as well as the customers and shareholders. The foundational commitments can be heard by all levels of the organization and, in fact, resonate particularly well with the front-line since the communication is so authentic.

Foundational Leaders

Foundational commitments provide guidance in turbulent times. They are like a compass. These bedrock commitments allow the leader to keep a sense of direction even when there is confusion and turbulence. While most wish that achieving extraordinary results and creating value could be orderly, predictable and stable, that simply is not the case. But foundational commitments do provide a sense of stability and guidance in the tough time

3.

Foundational Commitments – the Leader's Source

A leader is someone who makes things happen that would not otherwise happen. That is, the extraordinary occurs because of the impact this person has on others. To be a leader is to create what is needed to challenge, empower, guide and inspire others to accomplish the extraordinary. While it may not appear that the leader is especially gifted or charismatic, an impact is made on others. That impact leads to significant accomplishments. There are then the questions: Where does the leader get this "intangible" quality? How is it that the leader has this intangible quality and others do not? Said another way, "What is the source for a leader?"

Asking the question, "What is the source for a leader?" is a bit like asking, "What is the source for Superman?" That is, what gives Superman his powers? While you and I may have different memories of the explanation of Superman's powers based on which comic books we read and which cartoons and movies we saw, we are fortunate that today we can look on the Internet and get very detailed explanations. For example, "Since Superman is a native of Krypton, a planet that had a red sun, under a yellow sun (like that of Earth's), his Kryptonian cells act as living solar batteries, absorbing solar energy and giving him superhuman powers."   The various web sites devoted to Superman note that over time, in the various installments of Superman, the explanation of the source of his power changed slightly. This is ironic, since our understanding of what makes a leader has also changed over time with changes in the nature of the challenges facing businesses in an increasingly competitive global business environment.

Identifying what gives source to leaders is not so easily researched on the web. What we find on the Internet are many explanations and theories. These are what Gregory Batson referred to as "Explanatory Principles." An explanatory principle gives an explanation of something that we can use as a placeholder, but an explanatory principle actually gives little access to the phenomena. For example, if you hold your house keys out in front of you and then release them, the keys will fall to the floor. If I asked you why the keys fell to the floor rather than floating up in the air like a balloon, you would say, "Gravity" (and probably wonder what is wrong with me). Yet what does the explanation, "Gravity", actually tell us? Do we actually understand what the phenomenon is?

If we pushed this conversation further, you might say that what made the keys fall was the gravitational pull of the earth. This is a more advanced explanation (explanatory principle version 2), yet even this explanation does not give us any real understanding of the phenomena. Explanatory principles are useful as "placeholders." An explanatory principle makes something clearer by describing it, and yet the description does not provide access to knowledge. The good news is that we have a social convention to accept an explanation for those things that would otherwise get so complex that it would make us uncomfortable. Do most of us actually want to study physics in order to be able to genuinely understand why things fall to the earth? For most of us the answer is, "No thanks, I'm happy to leave that to the physicist. I'll stick with the explanation of gravity, rather than attempt to gain access to knowledge of the true complexity of gravity."

The same explanatory principles hold for leadership. We use the term very frequently, and the term does not actually lead us to learn or distinguish what is actually occurring when leadership occurs. As an example, if someone observed a work team that was performing markedly better than another and asked, "How come?", we might answer, "The reason this team is so successful is because of the leader." If that person then asked, "What does that statement mean?", we would say, "That person provided 'real leadership'." If pushed further, we might add, "This person has leader attributes", "This person acts like a leader", or "This person has leadership skills." If pushed further to explain where leaders get their power and strength we might say, "A leader is self-motivated" or "A leader gets strength from experience." I hope that you can see that all of those statements are examples of an explanatory principle. The statements give a description or explanation of something without actually providing access to what would allow one to produce similar extraordinary results from a group of people.

Given that you are reading this, I assume that you are interested in getting beyond the explanatory principle of leadership. To use the earlier

> *Foundational commitments are the source for leaders. Foundational commitments are the cornerstones for leaders who want what is best for the business.*

discussion on why keys fall to the floor as an analogy, we will move beyond the explanation of gravity (explanations of leadership) to understanding the physics (access to the source of leadership) involved.

Foundational Leaders

I assert that foundational commitments are the source for leaders. Foundational commitments are the cornerstones for leaders who want what is best for the business. This may include effective performance in a steady state, a bold change to achieve extraordinary results and sustainable transformation. Foundational commitments are the first step and the critical support on which everything else is built.

At this point you could be thinking. "OK, but what are foundational commitments and, oh, by the way, is this just another explanatory principle?" Those are great questions. First let's discuss the term "foundational commitments." I made up the term. There is no such thing as foundational commitments. If you conduct a CAT scan on a person who is widely acknowledged as a great leader, you will not see foundational commitments. You will not find any evidence of foundational commitments on the scan. I invented the term to try to distinguish, or at least point toward, the phenomena that I have seen occurring with individuals who impact groups of people to produce the extraordinary. I am using this invented term to force us to think differently than we have before about what happens when an individual interacts with a group of people so that extraordinary things occur. Later, I will describe what appears to be going on with an individual who is later called a leader. We will discuss how the leader appears to be "being", and how that way of "being" has such powerful impact on other people.

I have been privileged to consult with a large number of successful team leaders, managers and executives. I have

Those who achieve outstanding results have a common understanding that getting excellent results comes from unleashing the creativity, energy and tenacity of others.

noticed that those who achieve outstanding results have a common understanding that getting excellent results comes from unleashing the creativity, energy and tenacity of others. Further, they tend to have certain aspirations, beliefs, and tenets which impact how they look at situations, what they consider to be possible, which alternatives they choose, and how they communicate to others. It could be said that leaders have common commitments that are put into action. I am calling those commitments "foundational commitments" since they appear to be at the heart of who these leaders are being when they are performing their role and interacting with others.

In this following section, let's discuss in more detail the phenomena that is visible when we watch individuals whose behavior is later explained as "leadership." We will be looking at how these leaders' foundational commitments can be seen.

1. Being a Leader

> *The word "being" means "the nature or essence of a person". Foundational Commitments are the essence of a person whose being impacts others to accomplish the extraordinary.*

We use the word "being" to refer to the nature or essence of a person and the word "leader" to refer to a person who accomplishes the extraordinary through others.

> *The being of leaders orients who they are as persons in the face of the challenge facing the business.*

The first thing that I have noticed about successful leaders is that they are committed to being and doing whatever is required for the team and business to be successful. There is a burning passion for seeing that those around them are successful. In order to achieve this success, the leader is at-will to challenge, call out if need be, cajole, develop, encourage, remove blockages, provide resources, threaten, and train to see that the people are supported and succeed. Leaders take setbacks and losses personally, as if somehow they did not provide the direction, guidance, and support to have the team and business succeed. These commitments give rise to the being of the leader which, in turn, impacts the actions and speaking of the leader. Foundational commitments are the wellspring from which leaders draw their direction, energy, grounding and power to be effective leaders.

> *Foundational commitments are the source for being a leader. This is important because the being of a leader is the precursor to success as a leader.*

That is, a person is being a leader before any employees are impacted or results are achieved.

The being of a leader is what people ultimately come to trust or not. The trust of the employees is essential in that leaders make mistakes in what they say and do. Employees can overlook these mistakes and continue to trust the leader if they are confident in what the leader stands for and who the leader is being.

> *Being is where leadership begins. A person is being a leader before they ever do or say anything.*

A person's foundational commitments give rise to his or her being, which translates into acuity, clarity, direction, energy, passion and tenacity. These being-based attributes are perceived by their employees. The employees interpret this as evidence of a person who is authentic, competent and credible as a leader. In contrast, Situational Commitments give rise to a being of pseudo-leadership marked by personal aggrandizement, self-protection and self-centeredness. The employees clearly experience this as pseudo-leadership, and the employees behave accordingly. The consequences for the business are predictable and unfortunate.

2. Integrity

Leaders view their personal integrity as their most precious possession.

The definition of integrity is "the quality of having strong moral principles and the state of being whole." Leaders are exceedingly careful to act consistent with their moral principles, to behave consistent with their speaking, and to not mislead people through their actions and speaking. Rather, they challenge themselves to "walk the talk" in every thing they do. They take being one's word very seriously.

Integrity is one of those words that people are reluctant to use in business, yet it is at the heart of leadership. Leaders "be" that their word is their bond. Leaders "be" that "you can take my word to the bank and my handshake is my contract." This commitment to being integrity is at the heart of the foundational commitments and a key to what makes these leaders able to accomplish the extraordinary through their colleagues and employees.

> *Foundational Commitment leaders do not differentiate their behavior in their office with their behavior in front of the employees.*

They appreciate that others are watching every thing that they do, and they want to demonstrate their commitment in their actions as well as their words.

Another demonstration of being one's word is that people want to work around such a leader. There is a confidence and sense of trust that is very appealing. As demonstration of this, in my many years of consulting, I have never had the slightest "commercial problem" with a foundational commitment leader. I have never felt as if I was taken advantage of or had difficulty in collecting fees or had to deal with getting "beaten up on fees." That is not to say, these foundational commitment leaders do not complain about how high my fees are. They and I understand that I am committed to their being wildly successful and to my adding clear value to their work.

In contrast, I have also worked for a number of situational commitment pseudo-leaders. It is a striking contrast for me. In general, the pseudo-leaders listen for what they want to hear and are looking for ways to make themselves look good. Given that they have often "missed the plot" of what is going on in the business and organization, it is hard to support them in getting what they want, i.e., to look good without having to take risks and upset any of their "loyalists." In addition to being hard to work with, these pseudo-leaders are also notorious for commercial problems, i.e., challenging invoices to delay payments, being late in payments, etc. One of the first signs to me that I am dealing with a pseudo-leader comes from my accounting group who is having problems with collections for a contracted service for no apparent reason.

Changing Organizational Context

Leaders appreciate that the context for the business and team must change if significant accomplishment is to occur.

> *Leaders' Foundational Commitments will not let them continue to operate in a context that is not working. The organizational context is important in determining if the team will succeed, and so the leader continues to talk with others to find a way to articulate and invent the context that is needed for success.*

This context is essential to team performance since it determines how the employees see the circumstances and the opportunities that are presented to the team.

> *In contrast, the pseudo-leaders have been successful because of current or past context. Their interest is "getting back to the good old days."*

They often say, "We have done this before, and we know how to do this." They say this even when the performance is unacceptable. The pseudo-leader does not see the importance of context and would be unsuccessful even if they tried to create a new context.

Foundational Leaders

Being Unreasonable

> *A Foundational Commitment of leaders is to be unreasonable with themselves and others. This means these Foundational Commitment leaders do not accept excuses, explanation, and stories for why performance did not occur.*

They are unwilling to settle for all the good reasons why something cannot happen or be achieved. Leaders have learned to break up the stories and to keep pushing for a way to achieve the result. There is a tenacity to continue to challenge, based on a commitment to achieve results even when it is not yet clear how this achievement can be accomplished.

> *By contrast, pseudo-leaders who operate from Situational Commitments usually excel in explanations, excuses and stories.*

They can effectively describe why they think something happened. What they cannot effectively do is speak in such a way as to interrupt the excuses and stories. In addition, pseudo-leaders often get quite defensive, if not nasty, when their excuses and stories are challenged. This challenge is perceived as an affront and a treat to their intense desire to look good at all costs.

Evokes Energy

The foundational commitments of the leader are like Superman's Kryptonian cells. If you remember at the beginning of this chapter, we talked about Superman's Kryptonian cells acting as living solar batteries, absorbing solar energy and giving Superman superhuman powers. While the foundational commitments do not give superhuman powers, they do give the energy for accomplishing the extraordinary.

> *The leader's impact includes creating energy for those on the team and in the business.*

At the beginning, the leader will need to create or generate the clarity, direction, excitement and intensity that lead to others' creating their own energy. What allows the leader to create the initial burst of energy is the commitment and passion for the team's excelling, and for developing people. The key is to get the others on the team and in the business to be generate energy for themselves and others. It is the generation of energy by others that ultimately recharges the leader, as the earth's sun did for Superman's Kryptonian cells.

While the leader is generating energy to get the team moving, it is also a matter of concern that should be watched closely. Energy for the leader is often a most

> *"Energy and persistence conquer all things."*
> Benjamin Franklin

critical ingredient. Providing or generating the leadership to turn an organization, whether it is around or in a decidedly different direction, is a very challenging and demanding task. The leader experiences this challenge as very draining. Often a foundational commitment leader's main question is: "Do I have enough energy to get this done?"

In the early stages of a change, there is a particular demand or drain on energy. There are long hours, intense conversations and many meetings. In the early stages, the leader often has to generate the energy for the entire team, as well as for her or him. There is a demand for concentrated action and focus. The leader must be relentless in challenging, encouraging, confronting, demanding, and engaging. The challenge for the leaders is where does the energy come from? Of course, in part, it is from physical stamina, but the emotional and intellectual energy is actually sourced or charged/recharged from the leader's foundational commitments. This act of generation from foundational commitments is what sets the leader apart.

> *By contrast, pseudo-leaders often get their energy from fear, focus on survival and self-interest.*

While fear and survival will provide temporary bursts of energy, they are usually not sustainable. Attempts to lead teams to serve the self-interests of the leader usually are not successful, and the leader then resorts to demands for compliance and conformity. This, of course, will not move an organization to achieve successful change and sustainable results.

Overt Commitment

Part of the energizing of the others is their taking on the leader's commitments as their own. They may choose different words, yet the essence of the stand is the same. As an example, when Tom Stephens took over as CEO of Canada's largest forest products company, McMillan Bloedel, he told the employees that he was committed to three things:

> *The leader's overt commitments are the enactment or embodiment of Foundational Commitments. It is the articulation of "what I stand for," which is then translated into "what we as a team or business stand for."*

1. Safety – safest forest products company
2. Earning respect

3. Being outrageously successful

Those three items were Mr. Stephens' stand. They also were a bold statement of being a leader, as McMillan Bloedel was none of these at the time, and, in fact, was performing poorly in all three areas. However, within a short time, most employees could state the three parts of the CEO's stand as what the company was committed to. The stand shifted from the stand of the new CEO to the stand of the rank and file employees, which started the company on the road to becoming successful in all three areas.

I have noticed that leaders are able to take a stand in part out of their own personal desire to be committed to something and to working with people who come to share that commitment. In fact, leaders often gain great pleasure in watching others discover their own commitment to the team and business and then generate actions and accomplishments consistent with those commitments. There is great satisfaction in giving people something to believe in and then watching them perform in extraordinary ways. This is one area in which the leader's foundational commitments appear to be most reinforcing and rewarding. This engagement, in turn, will lead employees to take the actions needed to get the results for the business. The leader's stand is a deep commitment that shows through as the leader deals with the day-to-day business, as well as engages in conversations with employees.

> *The stand is the grounding from which the leader works. It gives a place of stability from which to develop a good perspective and contributes to developing the right perspective that will ultimately engage the employees.*

This stand supports the leader in demonstrating commitment. The stand provides valuable content as the leader demonstrates and discusses commitment. Valuable content is like the quality programming that is used on an entertainment channel. It is the rich, attracting content that will make employees pay attention and to connect to the commitment of the leader. It is demonstrable and can be seen by employees. In a conversation with an employee about how he knew that the plant manager was committed to certain outcomes, his reply would be, "I can see it. It is obvious." This obviousness in what engages employees and makes them want to follow and work with the leader.

Authentic Communication

> *One of the bedrock Foundational Commitments of a leader is to be in communication.*

This is not to say that leaders are always good at staying in communication; in fact, they struggle with it just as everyone else does. The difference is that they are committed to doing it even when they are not necessarily good at it. They find ways to support themselves in being in communication with others on the team and in the business.

This communication is consistent through everything the leader thinks, says, writes and does. Correspondingly, it is the key to the leader developing credibility with the employees based on how they listen to the leader. The Foundational

> *The leader's Foundational Commitment to be in communication is also reflected in an intense desire to be a better listener. Often leaders are aware that listening is critical for success; yet often listening is not one of their strongest skills.*

Foundational Leaders

Commitments are communicated and experienced by groups of employees. In change efforts a key conversation that occurs early is the discussion among the employees as to what the leader is up to. Invariably, there are questions: Can we trust this person? What is this person about? Ultimately am I interested in what this person is committed to? (One way I talk about this with my clients is to phrase this employee question as: Can I be enrolled in the future this person is committed to creating?) If the experience is that this person is committed to doing what is best for the business, even if it requires tough actions, employees will experience this and start to engage. If the commitment is personally to looking good, then the employees sense there is going to be just more of the same and ask themselves why they should be involved or contribute to any change the leader suggests. In fact, they often say to themselves, "I'll hunker down and protect what I've got. This new effort will pass, as new efforts have in the past."

The foundational commitment to being a good listener causes the leader to persist in developing advanced listening skills, which many business people today do not have. The ability to listen well is a critical skill for leaders. Most business people are much more comfortable talking than listening. There is an illusion of power when one is talking articulately and forcefully.

Too often, young leaders focus on saying the right thing and pay little attention to developing the skills to listen with great acuity. Employees will be engaged much more quickly when they know that their concerns and points of view are heard and appreciated by the leader than they would be engaged by a slick slide show or speech. Leaders often report that learning to listen well is among their highest challenges, and so having their foundational commitments energize the continued development of listening skills is essential. The leaders come to appreciate that their power actually comes from their ability to listen and learn. Listening allows access to the wants and needs of customers, employees, investors, suppliers, and other stakeholders.

The leader's foundational commitments also include providing a mechanism or structure with which to listen. The foundational commitment to listen results in some kind of clear structure for meeting with people in order to listen, for recording that listening, for repeating that listening back to the employee, etc. This structure works as a "listening device" for the comments and concerns of people on the team and in the organization. A central part of the increased skill in listening is the establishing of a commitment-based structure with which to listen: time, place, method, response, etc. This allows for heightened listening and for translating others' comments into expressions of the commitments of both the leader and the employees.

By listening intently to customers and employees, the leader is able to determine their commitment and concerns. This gives access to the areas in which they can be engaged and enrolled. Listening is a key to effective enrollment. Highly effective leaders come to attend to the commitment that is being spoken as much as the particular words that are being used.

> *Critical thinking begins with a sense of inquiry and questioning. There is a continual quest to better understand what is going on in the business and what the drivers are to improve performance. There is an unwillingness to settle for pat answers, stories, and excuses.*

Critical Thinking

The foundational commitment leader appreciates that critical thinking is a key enabler of success. Often the leader has to teach others to think, so that they can think critically.

A statement such as, "Well, everybody knows," provokes a leader with foundational commitments to question the thinking that is behind that statement. It is a bit like waving a red cape in front of an angry bull. Predictable responses will occur.

> *Critical thinking involves continuously challenging one's own thinking and the thinking of others. A leader appreciates that what has stopped a business from being successful is the myths and stories that the managers tell themselves.*

Getting the managers to challenge their own thinking to identify the myths is a key step in moving toward extraordinary results.

The consequence of not thinking critically is often noted by the expression: "What were they thinking?" After all the excuses and stories are told, the sad realization is that people simply were not thinking critically.

> *Thinking critically is not simply a matter of intelligence. Many very bright people with extensive education and experience are not effective in thinking critically.*

Thinking critically is not as common in businesses as one might think and certainly not as common as one would desire. There seem to be different reasons for this. First, in many companies a myth has developed that only managers, especially senior managers, are the people in the company who are supposed to think. It is common to have very experienced front-line workers tell graphic stories in which their attempts to add thinking to a discussion in their worksite was met with an instruction to "shut up and do what you are told." The tragedy of telling those closest to the work that they cannot add to the quality of thinking in their workplace has deprived shareholders of unthinkable amounts of value as well as taken the satisfaction of work away from many employees. A second factor in the limited level of critical thinking has been the heavy focus on getting tight processes.

> *The myth is that the process is fine, if we can just get the employees to execute it flawlessly. Rather than challenging the process, there is extreme attention to getting compliance.*

In compliance-oriented cultures, critical thinking is not appreciated. That is why employees are so eager to get with and support a leader who enables and encourages them to think critically about the business.

Situational commitment pseudo-leaders shut down critical thinking. They focus, instead, on avoiding any challenges to thinking that would make anyone uncomfortable or look bad.

> *By contract, pseudo-leaders with situational commitments spend enormous energy defending their history, the correctness of their answers, and complaining that their superiors would not be asking the questions they are asking if they understood the business.*

If a person has foundational commitments, these result in big commitments for the organization. The critical thinking process, then, will need to expand to get to the level and expanse required to develop a comprehensive understanding of the situation as well as courses or pathways of action.

Foundational Leaders

Leaders with foundational commitments are also more open to critical thinking that includes differences in points of view or different perspectives. They are more open to conversations and thinking differently from their own. There is a tolerance and appreciation of diversity and the power that different points of view can bring. Foundational commitment leaders usually surround themselves with people who are different in their thinking to assure that the proper challenges to the leader's thinking are made. These people who think a bit differently are often the ones who come up with the data and ideas that turn into extraordinary results. In contrast, people with situational commitments tend to surround themselves with loyalists who are agreeable, who usually have similar perspectives, and who will not challenge their thinking. At times it looks like a scene from an opera with the loyalists "singing choruses of praise" for the pseudo-leader.

Creating New Options

Possibility is a key to unlocking the power in teams

> *Possibility is the leader's secret weapon. Possibility is a way of getting people to open up and consider the alternatives.*

and organizations, and getting people engaged in improving the performance. It is the kind of conversation and questioning that so many employees want to have, and so many managers are afraid to have.

Create new options is a conversation about what could be accomplished, delivered or produced. In this kind of conversation there are no immediate constraints, restrictions, or critiques. There, of course,

> *Possibility invites a conversation of what could be.*

is a role for critique at some later time, but not in the early stages of conversations of creation and invention in thinking. Foundational commitments enable the leader to have confidence to think beyond the borders or boundaries of what is currently thought to be achievable.

In business lingo there is an expression, "thinking outside the box." This expression is best illustrated by a graphic where nine dots are drawn on a piece of paper or whiteboard. The person is then instructed to connect all nine of the dots by drawing four straight lines without lifting the pencil or pen.

If you have not seen this demonstration, try it:

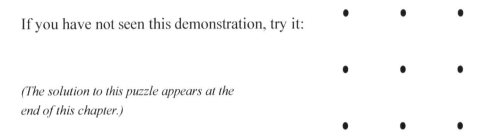

(The solution to this puzzle appears at the end of this chapter.)

The point of this demonstration is that the mind sees an imaginary "box" when it sees the nine dots. Is there a box there? No, but the mind acts as if there is and set boundaries and parameters on what is possible. The mind shapes what we see as possible when we look at the nine dots and, in turn, shapes what is seen as possible actions and solutions. In similar ways business people may be limited in their view of the circumstances, customer behavior, competitive forces, market conditions, etc. There are "nine dots" and imaginary boxes around their part of the business. If these imaginary boxes are not interrupted, the boxes will dramatically reduce what people can see as possible. A leader with foundational commitments, however, continues to seek out the possibility that exists and can be explored and does not allow conversations to be limited by "nine dot imaginary boxes." The leader, then, provides the energy and intensity to continuously challenge "the box," whether it is the perceived limits of performance, approaches, or the contribution that employees can make to the business.

Increased level of critical thinking comes from the leader being able to see a full range of possibilities. The leader's personal commitments and stand give access to a whole range of possible options. "We can't" is not a familiar expression of a leader. Rather it is "we will" or "we will keep looking until we find a way." The critical thinking of the foundational commitment leader will continue to focus on exploring for further options. The commitments are experienced most powerfully as new options. Creating new options is expansive, as it leads to the question of "What would fulfilling these options that we have seen from critical thinking allow us to do that we don't see as possible today?"

While ultimately there are boundaries on what is acceptable to consider, the act of critical thinking, nonetheless, becomes an enabler. As an example, if a leader has a foundational commitment of respect for employees and safety, those possibilities that would put employees at great harm will not be acted upon. However, since the leader has clarity or sharpness in perspective, there will be more resourcefulness available.

I have noticed that as leaders grow and mature, their relationship to creating new options expands. It becomes not only something that is useful and expresses their commitment, but actually becomes a commitment in and of itself. There is a joy that the leader sees in what people do when they discover their own possibilities, and this is rewarding in and of itself. It is the possibility of what can be contributed to others. The satisfaction of this contribution and gift is very rewarding to the leader.

A person with situational commitments has little facility with possibility, since their field of view of what is possible is restricted to that which will assure that their appearance is enhanced. If the only things that a leader can consider are those which will make her/him look good or at least avoid looking bad, the conversation of what is possible is dramatically reduced.

Foundational Leaders

Focus on Excellence in Implementation

A foundational commitment for leaders is excellence in implementation. This translates to wanting to do what is right and an intense focus on doing what is necessary for success. The leader is focused on implementation because that is the key to success. The "game" is won or lost in implementation, and the deep commitment to the success of the business and the people drives the leader to keep a keen eye on the key drivers of success in implementation.

In contrast, pseudo-leaders with situational commitments do not excel at implementation, especially strategic implementation. By that I mean implementation of something that involves risk or is in someway not completely predictable. Pseudo-leaders do not show a commitment to excellence in implementation if that implementation requires real leadership rather than merely managing and overseeing the unfolding of what predictably will happen. Leadership is making something happen that was not going to happen, and this is scary ground for a pseudo-leader. In fact, as I have thought about it, I think pseudo-leaders are unable to see the possibility or opportunity for such a bold move and therefore, cannot think their way through strategic implementation. The field of view what is possible is restricted to options that are designed to enhance the pseudo-leader's image. The cost of "imagine enhancement" is a narrowed range of view, with no access to the very paths that would create success. The commitment to looking good is greater that the commitment to getting the result. For pseudo-leaders the commitment to looking good and having an organization full of loyalists who surround the pseudo-leader results is so strong that attempts to point toward it and/or break it up are almost always resisted. It appears that the only thing that will bring this commitment to looking good to an end is the lack of business results. The lack of business results appears to be the only force strong enough to disrupt it.

A consequence of having a pseudo-leader is that implementation will always be limited to that which is predictable. Given that simply doing what is predictable or safe is not appropriate for many businesses today, having a pseudo-leader in a key position is an extreme limitation. Perhaps governmental agencies and the Post Office tolerate this. But when we think about the poor performance in the Post Office and the debacle with FEMA in Katrina, perhaps we would decide that such limitations are not acceptable even in organizations like the Post Office and agencies of our government. Perhaps as I think about it, this may explain some of what drives the creation of bureaucracy in companies and government. Perhaps these organizations are led by pseudo-leaders whose commitment is to protect themselves, to look good and not be shown up to look bad.

Courage

The leader also has the courage to declare and confront interruptions to the intended actions. "When the going gets tough the tough go shopping" is not a description of a foundational commitment leader. Rather, when the going gets tough, true leaders go back to their foundational commitments.

Foundational Commitments will not allow the leader to hide out, be politically correct, or put personal career safety ahead of what is best. Rather, the leader will have the courage to take risks and to encourage the team to take the risks necessary to be successful.

By contrast the situational commitment pseudo-leader focuses on what is politically correct and does everything possible not to take personal risks. This pseudo-leader will let others get out on the limb and will sacrifice as many employees as necessary to continue to look good.

Foundational Leaders

In Conclusion

Foundational commitments are the source for leaders. Like the Krypton cells that were the strength for Superman, these foundational commitments provide the energy and power for the leader. These commitments shape the being of the leader. This is important because being a leader is the precursor to having an impact on others and to achieving success. These "being"-based attributes are watched carefully by employees and are at the heart of the credibility and rapport that leaders develop with others. This credibility and rapport open the door for leaders to interact in unique ways, and it is through these interactions with foundational commitment leaders that teams and businesses accomplish the extraordinary. They make something happen that was otherwise not going to happen. This leadership will in turn assure the continued achievement of excellent results.

Foundational commitment leaders are tenacious in protecting their integrity and being that their word is their bond. They create a new context for the team, one that gives the team access to actions that they otherwise would not have. The leader communicates a personal stand for success, which, over time, is adopted by the team. The leader learns to listen and provides a definitive structure for listening to employees. The leader asks for critical thinking

The Leader's Source:
1. Foundational Commitments
2. Being a leader
3. Being one's word
4. Context modified
5. "Unreasonable" or not accepting excuses
6. Evoking energy
7. Overt commitments
8. Authentic communication
9. Critical thinking
10. Gives access to new possibility
11. Courage

from all employees. The foundational commitment leader is unreasonable about the team finding a way to be successful and will not accept excuses and stories.

Key to the Dot puzzle:

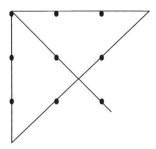

Foundational Leaders

4.

Foundational Commitments in Action

Leadership occurs in action. Leadership is action that produces additional action in others.

Strategic execution is predicated on action. Not just any old action, but inspired actions of others to produce extraordinary results. Effective leadership is based on the commitments and values of the leader(s). Inspired actions of others can be thought of as a reaction to or in response to the actions of leaders. The evidence for effective leadership actions is the effective actions of others. Leadership is not fixed or a static phenomenon. Instead it is very dynamic and being fine tuned to increase the quality of actions from others.

Building on Foundational Commitments

> *Commitment without action is wasted.*

Commitment without action is wasted. In fact, if commitments are not manifested in actions, there are serious questions about the depth and validity of the commitment. From time to time we all have good ideas and "shoulds." "I should lose weight, I should exercise more frequently, I should floss my teeth more regularly, I should get more sleep, and etc. All of these are good things for us to do. It is easy to say we are committed to these things, and yet more difficult to alter our patterns.

If we say we are committed but do not put actions in place to alter our behavior, we are not authentically committed. The distinction of foundational commitments is that these commitments are so strong for these people that they can not help but put them into action. Further, the need to express and act is so strong that from time to time leaders put these actions into place even though it is immensely unpopular with their colleagues.

Inspiring others to excel is what Foundational Leaders do. Seeing people being inspired and taking action is among the highest reward to leaders. These leaders enjoy seeing others get turned on to the business and then go about achieving "outrageous things". The leader's foundational commitments show up in a leader's actions, attitudes, communications, decisions and etc. The "proof" of a leader's foundational commitments is the inspired actions of others that translated to performance of the team and organization.

In contrast, pseudo-leaders often become concerned if other employees become "too inspired" and go after extraordinary results. The pseudo-leader's concern is that dramatic increases in performance will make them look bad. Pseudo-leaders are motivated to look good at all cost, and are very upset with things that could make them look bad. The threat of others accomplishments is hard to understand, but yet is quite real to the pseudo-leaders.

Foundational Leaders

In this chapter we will look at how Foundational Leadership turns into actions for strategic execution. These are value creating actions taken by employees in response to the impact and influence of leaders. The bottom line is that if you watch a leader closely you will see certain behaviors, interactions and patterns of results that set that person apart from the non-leader or pseudo-leader. In this chapter we will look at the specific behaviors and the interactions that produce inspired actions of others and business results. But first, let's look at other parallels between Superman and leaders.

Parallels of Superman

In an earlier chapter, I discussed the parallels in source of power between Superman and leaders. We looked at what was the source for Superman, or what gave him his power. We found the explanation to be his Kryptonian body cells that were recharged by the yellow rays of the earth's sun. In contrast we discussed that the leader's source is foundational commitments, which are "recharged" by the impact of others. The "mythical sun" that recharges leaders is the glow that comes from people's faces. The glow occurs as people accomplish results that were previously thought to be very difficult if not impossible. The thrill of watching individuals, teams and parts of the organization accomplish the extraordinary is what energizes true leaders.

In this chapter I will discuss with you what leaders do. Interestingly there are some parallels in what Superman did with his power and what leaders do with theirs.

- Superman used his strength to achieve remarkable feats. Leaders use their capacities to achieve remarkable feats.

- Another similarity is that for the majority of the time Superman was a "mild mannered reporter" who did not seek to call attention to himself.

While many leaders are not necessarily "mild mannered", they do not go out of their way to call attention to themselves. Rather they prefer to call attention to the business and team, and to the accomplishments that are being achieved by the employees. While true leaders are not prone to call attention to themselves, that cannot be said of pseudo-leaders. Actions that call attention to oneself is a common characteristic of a pseudo-leader.

- Perhaps the most interesting difference between Superman and a leader is that Superman's achievements came through his personal actions while leader's achievements come through actions of others. Leaders produce *inspired actions of others* to accomplish the extraordinary.

What Foundational Leaders Do That Sets Them Apart

Foundational Leader's actions reflect their Foundational commitments. This is because their foundational commitments form the context for them as leaders. The context gives meaning to all that occurs around them, and shapes what they see in the business. What the leaders can

1. **Quality of preparation**
2. **Quality of the people "on the team"**
3. **Interactions of the team**
4. **Ability to anticipate, see what is happening and react appropriately and quickly**
5. **Flawless execution**
6. **Velocity**
7. **Results**

see shapes the range of potential actions as well as the action that is taken. Some actions are unique to the leader and others are unique to the particular situation. However, the overall pattern of actions is what I am interested in discussing with you. I say that the following categories of action are reflective of foundational commitments being expressed.

As I discuss these categories, I will use analogies from sports which I think will make these discussions more vivid for you.

Intense Preparation

If you watch sports, you have undoubtedly heard about the intense preparation of the best coaches and players. The National Football League (American professional football) provides a good example. The best coaches are the best strategist. Their single focus is what strategies can be used to beat their opponent's strategies. The

> *Change and growth take place when a person has risked himself and dares to become involved with experimenting with his own life.*
> Herbert Otto

coaches spend many hours studying films of their upcoming opponents. They develop schemes of actions that they think will bring success in all aspects of the game (offense, defense, special teams).

The players also spend many hours studying the players they will be opposing in the upcoming game. In some cases it is a one-on-one match, like a defensive end vs. an offensive tackle. In other cases it is much more complicated, like the different approaches to coverage in the secondary that receivers can anticipate. The most intense preparation is from the quarterback on the offense and the counterpart on the defense (usually a middle line backer). Intense preparation is essential. Often the players and teams that are the best prepared are the most successful at execution during the game.

The NFL players have spent many years building their strength and skills to be able to play at this high level. Most started playing the game when they were little boys and have played it throughout high school and university. Their personal preparation has been most of their life time. Further, they must continue to do physical conditioning and working on the skills required of their position throughout the year. There is very little slacking off if they are to excel.

Self-development

> *Leaders have worked hard on developing themselves.*

Foundational Leaders are like NFL football coaches and players. Leaders have worked hard on developing themselves. This intense participation includes preparing their personal lives. They have designed their lives to support their work. Their homes are designed to support the leader resting, thinking and working. Their partners/spouses (and children if applicable) understand the importance of the leaders' work. They understand (although not always like) the leaders' personal commitments to excellence in their jobs.

Most spend their lifetime dealing with their personal characteristics that if left unaltered, will interfere with

> *Leaders have developed a solid understanding of what drives them as well as the characteristics and tendencies that will not work.*

their effectiveness as a leader. This preparation also involves being honest about prior experiences. This is particularity important to understand in times in which they behaved badly or failed. This introspection is often painful. These personal challenges and pain have sharpened the leader's appreciation of the struggle of others, and of the difficulties encountered in producing significant change in an organization.

They have spent most of their lives leading others and looking for ways to improve their effectiveness as leaders. They spend hours building their skills and strengths as leaders. Many have had coaches and mentors that supported them in being better leaders.

As these leaders move into positions where they can execute strategy and transformation, they continue to work as hard. Leaders intensely prepare. Leaders are excellent in preparing for the challenges that come next. Further, they develop themselves for their roles. They are committed to excellence in management as well as leadership. They bring discipline and rigor to the workplace. Leaders tend to work hard and for long hours. Seldom do they have low handicaps in golf or "well balanced" personal lives. The task of preparation for leadership becomes a top priority.

Personal Motives Include Value Creation

The leader's intense preparation is to assure value creation from the strategic execution. Value creation is the reason the business exists and what an executive /manager is expected to do. The leader's personal motivations take a back seat to value creation.

Inspiring Others

Employees appreciate the preparation of their leaders. It shows up as evidence that the leader is serious about the role and prepared to be successful in the role. This intense preparation is one of the first areas of credibility for employees coming to trust a person as a leader.

Evidence of Intense Preparation to Lead

- Integrity
- Value creation
- Personal motives above question
- Inspiring others
- Well being of others

Preparation of Pseudo-leaders

In contrast, pseudo-leaders are often not intensely prepared for the challenges of leading a transformation. Pseudo-leaders are often surprised by the situations as they start to unfold and rather bewildered as to how this happened and what to do next. They have not done the hard personal work prior to the assignment and are unable or unwilling to do what is needed to "catch up". As a result, pseudo-leaders are often perceived by their employees as ill-prepared and not being up to the difficult challenges, and someone not to be trusted or followed.

Quality of the team

Sport teams are built by picking the right players and then developing them. In the NFL and NBA, the annual draft is a major event. Teams open their facilities so that fans can come in and watch the proceedings. Draft decisions are incredibly important to building a winning team. The draft decisions are made after months and months of study. The teams send scouts to watch the games, talk with coaches and other players. The scouts have formal and informal sessions in which the players demonstrate their speed, strength and skills. In addition, the coaches dissect the game films of the prospective draft choices for as many years as there is film available. The coaches then attempt to determine how that player's skill will fit with the strategies of the team. An increasingly important factor in draft decisions is the person's character and personal history. If the person's history is one of being difficult to coach and prone to discipline problems, then that history becomes a substantial dynamic in the decision process.

Leaders also know how critical it is to have the best players on their team, and act accordingly. Leaders look for skills as well as character. Selecting "players" with foundational commitments is essential, and it is equally important to deselect "players" with Situational Commitments.

Quality of Team Shown in Creativity and Generation

In athletics, the quality of a team is demonstrated by creativity and generation. In watching English football (soccer in the US), a recurring comment is that a winning team had many fresh ideas. These ideas are what allowed the team to break down the defenses of the opposing team. Finding players who have fresh ideas is essential as a sporting team is developed. This applies to business teams, where the leaders are looking for colleagues who have fresh ideas for strategic execution and transformation.

"Generate" is a term that I hear used frequently in NFL games. Typically it is that the defense needs to generate a turnover. That is, the defense needs to take the ball away from the other team and either score a touchdown or at least give the ball to their team's offense in a very advantaged location on the field. In business, a leader creates or generates leadership as needed. The foundational commitments are in action as leadership is made present even when it is not coming from other parts of the organization. The leader creates conversations that guide and inspire employees to think and act in a new way. The leader shows up for employees as a breath of fresh air, or a bit confronting.

Interactions of the Team

Communication

Being in communication is a foundational commitment that most leaders have, and it shows up in their intense focus on seeing that effective communication is occurring throughout the team(s) and organization.

Interactions
1. Communication
2. Credibility
3. Authenticity
4. Express Commitment
5. Create Possibility for Change
6. Declare Future Control

Leaders understand the extreme importance of communication. Communication is the medium of leaders. It is how they impact others and is at the heart of everything that a leader does. Not all leaders are terrific communicators. Some are quite reserved and shy. However, when they do communicate it has power and impact on others.

Credibility

Talking about the future is a crucial aspect of leadership. Having the credibility with the employees so that they will listen is a key to effective leadership. The credibility with employees is a reflection of their appreciation of the leader's foundational commitments. The leader's foundational commitments provide energy and intensity to the leader's speaking. The commitments are also expressed in the leader's actions. All of this contributes to the employees coming to have confidence and trust in the leader. Until a leader has established credibility with the employees, little meaningful change will be achieved.

One of the biggest challenges facing supervisors and managers today is credibility with their employees. I think this comes, in part, from the experience people in the organization have with a number of managers who are blatantly self-serving and telling the employees whatever they think will serve their own self-interest. This is contrasted to the leader who will "shoot straight" and tell you everything they can tell you. In particular, talking with employees about areas of uncertainly and possible risk to them personally. This authenticity in the behavior and communication of the leader is what sets them apart. By contrast, the person who tries to say and do all the "right things" will invariably be caught in a web of contradictions. This web is more easily seen than most managers want to believe, and leaves people in the organization suspicious of the candor, honesty and motives of the manager.

Authenticity

A leader is always concerned with "being authentic", and not being "phony or inauthentic". Foundational commitments give authenticity and candor to the speaking of the leader, and make the communication about the need for change land well with the employees. Foundational commitments are experienced at all levels of the organization, and in fact resonate particularity well with the front-line employees, since it is so authentic.

> *In working with younger leaders, the challenge is to have them get it touch with what is absolutely true for them, and not be too concerned with what others may think.*

There is a tendency to want to say, or at least "spin" the message so that it lands well with the listener and includes some of what the listener wants to hear. The more experienced and effective leaders have learned to speak from their heart with little concern for "sugar coating" or fear of how it may be heard. If the leader is authentically committed to what is best for the business and committed to the safety and well being of the employees, the core message will come through and reach the employees in a special way.

Expressing Commitment

Commitment can be difficult to communicate. Too often there is a desire to describe the communication, rather than to speak it. A described communication usually has a hollow feel. It is also indicative of a person with situational commitments. A leader with foundational commitments speaks, and his or her commitments become clear in their speaking. It is not that these leaders are necessarily more skilled in use

> *Commitment simply "shows itself" in the actions / speaking of the leader.*

of language. Rather it is that the commitment simply "shows itself" in the actions/speaking of the leader. What allows this to occur is that foundational commitments are "invented conversations", i.e., they are conversations that leaders have with themselves and with everyone around them. These conversations provide the energy and possibility for others to see and better understand the current circumstances as well as changes that are needed.

There is an important interaction that occurs between a person's foundational commitments and a person's thinking and actions. Given the striving for continual improvement and winning, the leader is always actively challenging his/her own thinking, looking for an additional clarity and a better way to think/look at the challenges facing the business.

Creating the Possibility for Change

Leaders create possibility for others. There is both an inspiration and a motivation to reach beyond what is certain and comfortable. The power or source for creating these possibilities comes directly from the leader's foundational commitments.

> *The foundational commitments are translated into a view of the future and what is possible for the business that does not necessarily come from the circumstances of the business. Rather it comes from what the leader is committed to, and is willing to be accountable for achieving with others in the business.*

The created possibility is empowering to people in the business as it enlarges the possibility that the employees can see for their contribution to the business. In many cases the employees feel that they have been given minimal opportunity to make an impact; and, in many cases, have felt betrayed, if not punished, for attempting to contribute to the business.

Declaring the Context for the Future of Business

As it turns out, context is the decisive factor in achieving extraordinary results. Context is the invisible premises that affect how the employees see the business and the opportunities that are available. Often there are many opportunities for improving performance that the employees simply do not see as a result of the existing context. To make the changes that are required to achieve extraordinary performance usually requires a change in context. Changing the context calls for leadership. Since the context is so comfortable and familiar, employees cannot be counted on to see the existing context not identify the new one absent leadership. There is an old saying that the three unknowns are; air to the bird, water to the fish, and man to himself. We could add a fourth, the context to the people in the business.

The possibility of a new context comes as an expression of the leaders commitments. That is, the commitments shape what the leader can see as possible in the future for the business. The seeing of what is possible for the future also enables the seeing of the existing context. In summary, the new context is essential, in that without it, there is little hope of achieving extraordinary results.

Ability to Anticipate, See What Is Happening and React Appropriately and Quickly

The game is when all of the preparation is put to the test. Each of the coaches is constantly communicating with the other coaches and the quarterbacks through headsets. The intent of the communications is to figure out what the opposition is doing.

Bias for Action

Leaders have a bias for action. The leader is prone to action and to want to see others in the organization in action as well.

Talk about the Future, Not Just the Past

A leader's role in the organization is to create actions and results that would otherwise not happen for the people on teams and in the business. Change implies that something different occurred than what was expected and given by the past. The leaders' talking about the future is a crucial aspect of leadership. It is through the leaders talking that the employees come to see that something is possible that they had not seen before. Further, they come to see that by collaboration they could accomplish what was previously not thought possible.

Tenacity

Leaders show a determination and toughness to keep moving and inventing in order to achieve business results. Foundational commitments are key to having the tenacity to keep leading even in the face of strong obstacles in order to get the results. That is, it is often said that it is "darkest just before dawn." This is a vivid description of what the leader who is going after a transformation often experiences. There is usually strong opposition from inside the company to the change, and there are numerous opportunities for the leader to get disheartened and "back off". However, at the end of the day, what the leader is committed to is sufficiently strong as to keep her or him "plugging away" until the result is achieved.

> *The fundamental commitments of the leader and the passion for excellence in performance lead to dissatisfaction with the current performance and status quo.*

Establishing Candor and Clarity about Current Condition

While others in the organization will try to convince the leader that things are better than they appear, etc., the leader is convinced that change is needed. This leads to conversations about the current condition and level of performance of the business. Often some on the management team perceives the candor and clarity as "unpleasant" conversations. There is an attempt to say that things are not as bad as described or that there is a good excuse/explanation. The denial along with the desire to blame circumstances and others makes it difficult to get accountability clear and an accurate assessment completed.

Foundational commitments are expressed by the leader, and allows for some to make the transition beyond the denial and deflections. Those who cannot make the transition are usually not around when the extraordinary results are achieved.

Flawless Execution

Identifying Metrics and Outcomes

Leaders are committed to achieving results. There is a rigorous focus on identifying the right kind of results, and then to achieving a level of results that will give the business an attractive competitive position. In addition, the identification of results to which the leader is committed is a key to establishing credibility with the employees. Outcomes make commitments seem real.

> *Metrics are essential to achieving extraordinary results in performance. Metrics tell the organization what is important, since it is what will be measured. If the same metrics are in place, it is usually a signal that little has changed.*

Thus leaders find it important to rigorously interrogate the metrics to see if they are pulling for the proper behavior, and inspiring the employees' behavior. Challenging existing metrics often takes courage and tenacity, and this is fueled by the leaders' foundational commitments.

Aligning on the Actions

Leaders with foundational commitments understand that until there is alignment on plans of action, nothing has happened other than talking. Also, there is a sharp focus on getting accountabilities clear.

Employees' being in action is the key to successful implementation of change. Further, it is usually the front-line workers who hold the keys to success or failure. Successful change will not come from trying to tell these front-line employees what to do. That is more of the same, and likely what got the business in the current predicament. Substantial change will be best achieved through engaging these front-line workers in identifying the solutions and implementing them. Usually they can identify and implement needed changes much more quickly than others. However, if that is the case, how come they are often so reticent to act? I think it is because they are so skilled at identifying the difference between foundational commitment and situational commitments. They are very aware that managers with situational commitments will not serve them in the long run and will not get the needed results.

Tenacious with Interruptions

As stated above, enrolling employees and dealing with interruptions are the paving stones for the road to extraordinary performance. An interruption is declared when someone discovers a gap between the promised actions and the current performance or trajectory. While business teams may appreciate the concept of interruptions providing opportunity, there is nonetheless a tendency to want to deny its existence and ignore the possible consequences. Often there is a strong pull not to acknowledge the interruptions. This is where the foundational commitments come in, and have the leader do what is needed and right, rather than what is poplar. In addition, this same drive prevents settling on superficial explanations for the cause of the interruptions.

A leader's foundational commitments are experienced or seen by employees. It is also seen when the foundational commitments are not strong or clear. The actions of employees are usually consistent with the absence of foundational commitments. There are excuses and stories for why things didn't work out or happen as expected. Also, the absence of authentic and clear commitments translates into fear and anxiety in the team or business.

Persisting In Action Until Results Are Achieved

An outcome of foundational commitments is a steadfast attention to accomplishment and an unwillingness on the part of the leader to settle for anything less. The foundational commitments provide an always-available, special energy and focus for the on-going challenge that the leader experiences personally and sees experienced in the environment. Foundational commitments then show up as drive and tenacity for the leader, at the same time that they show up as a source for creating opportunities for others.

Another manifestation of foundational commitments is that the leader is always wary of the pull to complacency. The leader is aware that one of the biggest threats to success in implementation is people getting comfortable and complacent prior to the results being achieved. The leader uses the language of foundational commitments to energize when the slogging gets hard or people start to settle for less than the change promises.

Foundational Leaders

Changing the Organizational Culture

The key to transformation is that the end point is to have an organization that is outcome based. That is, the primary commitment of the organization is achieving promised outcomes. While it would seems that this would be how most organizations are designed, that is not the case. Most organizations are designed to maintain control and to having efficient processes, with the assumption that the existing processes and procedures will achieve an acceptable level of results. This is contrasted with the organization that starts with the commitment to excellent results and then works to find how it can be achieved inside of acceptable controls and processes.

Changing the culture involves determining what is in the foreground, and in the background. Commitment to achieving results and values of the company are in the foreground, with proper controls and process integrity in the background. It is the belief of where to start and what will actually lead to success.

Given that the already existing conversation in most organizations are command and control process refinement, and the corresponding avoiding of domination by employees … collaboration around outcomes that will benefit all is the place to start. This makes the importance of generation of leadership even more critical if the organization is to focus on results and mobilizing employees to achieve those results.

Engaging Employees
The road to extraordinary performance is paved with the engagement of employees and willingness to deal with interruptions. Engagement happens only when the employees choose. That is, employees become engaged in the future and possibility for the business that the leader(s) have articulated. Many managers

approach their employees by telling them what to do. While this is satisfying to the manager's ego, it will not produce extraordinary results. Extraordinary results come only when employees have come to see what is in it for themselves and their part of the business.

A leader's foundational commitments are demonstrated through speaking and actions. This provides credibility with the employees. Most employees are actually quite willing to be led and want to contribute. Foundational commitments allow the leader to connect with the employees, and in time to engage and enroll them in the changes that are required and in developing the actions needed to implement the change.

In addition, these foundational commitment sourced conversations provide the employees with the opportunity to assess the leader to determine if they can trust this person and want to risk becoming involved in the change effort. As the change efforts unfold, the leader's commitments will also provide the employees with an opportunity to discover their own foundational commitments and ultimately to generate their own unique expressions of leadership. When individual employees begin taking a risk and generating from their own foundational commitments is when "magic" begins to happen in large change efforts. This magic includes the achieving of significant business results.

What Employees Look for in a Leader

Employees look for clues and evidence as to what kind of a person is their potential team leader, manager or executive. They are looking to see if this person is authentic, competent, compassionate, and trustable. They are looking to see if this is a person they should consider as a leader and engage with. As discussed previously, if the team leader or manager has foundational commitments, it will show up in how the person is being which in turn translate into actions and behaviors. This is what the employees' experience, and leads to their viewing the person as a leader and being willing to join with them in making something happen.

Most employees are skilled at reading the intention and commitments of their managers, as well as their local labor leaders if the employee is involved with a union. What do the employees see? I assert that they see the leaders' foundational commitments. An example, leaders insist on the highest level of integrity and set that standard for others in the organization. Further, leaders are shocked if they discover that their sales people are accepting orders for products that are not in stock and cannot be manufactured within the time frame promised to the customer. The employees notice what the leader identifies as a problem as well as the response of the leader to the situation. The employees also watch to see if the leader understands the key drivers of the business, e.g., metrics and how the leader responds. The employees will be positively impacted if they see that the leader is shocked to discover that a logistics group uses metrics to make their own performance look good while knowing that the actual impact on the customer is quite negative. If the leader steps up to address the problem, the employees will take note. If the pseudo-leader gives an explanation for the metrics and protects the logistics manager, the people will also take note.

Employees want their leaders to insist that the organization is doing the right things and doing them in proper manner. This builds much credibility for the leader. Employees also want to see that their leaders also look for every opportunity to develop the capability of each employee and the organization. If employees were asked to commit to the team and organization, they would like

> *"A man's own good breeding is the best security against other people's ill manners."*
>
> Lord Chesterfield

to see the organization also commit to developing them so that they can have a future with the business.

Employees are also skilled at reading managers and union officers who have Situational Commitments. These pseudo-leaders insist on doing what is expedient in a situation, not necessarily what is right. In the examples given above the pseudo-leader is more concerned with hitting the sales plan and maximizing bonuses than any negative impact or upset with the customer. Employees understand that the pseudo-leader will do whatever is necessary to look good. Most employees will interpret this kind of behavior as being negative for the business, and not trust the pseudo-leader.

Velocity

The leader is often bold in action and not complacent about waiting for others. Leaders often describe themselves as "not patient", and this is reflective, of their commitment to getting the results, being unwilling to listen to excuses and unwilling to tolerate long delays in action because others do not know what to do or do not want to take distasteful actions. Leaders are aggressive in doing what is right for the business. Pseudo-leaders are often aggressive in doing what is best for them. Pseudo-leaders are often quite aggressive, but in the wrong areas.

The leader has a high sense of urgency and appreciation for the importance of initiating the needed actions to get things moving. The leader will often be worried about maintaining momentum and velocity even when it appears that the change is unfolding nicely. In contrast, pseudo-leaders are often not urgent. This seems to come from belief that things will work out ok if we just give it a bit more time, as well as needing to check out if the proposed actions will be acceptable to their loyalists.

Results

A pattern of outstanding business results is the best indication of the presence of a leader. In watching leaders over time what you see is that they move into a position, and in a short period of time there is an up tick in activity followed by a notable improvement in results. This has happened repeatedly and all but predictably.

Perhaps the best way to spot leaders who operate with strong foundational commitments is to look at the track record of the results of the person's team/unit *and* the caliber of the people around them in the organization. A manager with Situational Commitments is often the manager who has a spotty track record of results but is described as having "enormous potential," along with a good explanation for the gaps in performance. Another indicator of Situational Commitments is management who micromanage their employees and drive the organization through fear and intimidation.

Leaders with foundational commitments on the other hand usually have a track record of outstanding results in different parts of the product and price cycle. Another sign that foundational commitments are present is if the person has built a very strong organization in which there are bright, talented people with strong personalities. And if there is the sense of contention, as the people continue to challenge themselves and their peers, this is an even better sign. In the end, continued achievement of outcomes and continued ability to lead and motivate talented teams is the best evidence of foundational commitments.

Employees Achieving the Outrageous

My firm had the privilege of working with Ford Motor Company during the difficult times of the 1980s. Following the successful turnaround, my partners and I were often asked, "Where were the secrets to Ford's success." One of the answers that rings as true for me today as in those years when we were working with Ford is this: there were Ford leaders who had a *foundational commitment* that Ford would not fail. These leaders had such strong foundational commitments to the success of their company that they produced extraordinary result after extraordinary result until their company again became highly successful.

One particular example comes to mind. A small group of engineers at Ford were so committed to the success of a particular product that they decided to do something outrageous. Sales of this particular car model were declining. It was viewed by consumers as an uninspiring model, even being described as an "underpowered grandmother's car." These courageous engineers, acting out of their foundational commitment that Ford Motor Company not fail, decided to take a risk and see if they could help the company by saving this car. The engineers decided to add a big engine to the model and attempt to sell the car to local police and state highway patrols. This seemed unlikely, since it was standard practice for police cars to be four-door models. The car model in question was a two-door and not even a "full-sized" model. However, undaunted, the engineers worked with an "after market" shop in Detroit and built up demos of the car with large powerful engines and shipped them to law enforcement conferences and tradeshows. To much surprise, the demo was a hit and substantial orders were received. Armed with this success, the engineers did more tinkering with the model, and the large engine version was made available to the general public. The car in question was the Ford Mustang, which became a widely popular model and revolutionized the consumer's view of cars from Ford.

The large-scale change in Ford that constituted the company's turnaround was led by individuals like the engineers of the Ford Mustang, who acted - against all odds - out of their foundational commitments. An interesting aspect of foundational commitments is that people around a leader can see these commitments and be inspired to act in alignment with the commitments. So it is not the well-guarded secret it may appear to be. Rather, it is front and center in how people relate to their leaders, even if the term *foundational commitment* is not used. The people around the leader are engaged by the authenticity of the commitment and the leader. This will be expressed as "He's the real deal" or "I'd follow that woman anywhere." In these comments is the acknowledgement that there is something in the leader's being and the leader's conversations that is authentic and that enrolls the person and the group. It is this enrollment that produces the inspired actions and then, in turn, the business results.

Conclusion

In conclusion, Foundational Leaders demonstrate foundational commitments through their "walking and talking", and it shows up in the people around them. While the personality and style of leaders is quite different, the actions that come from foundational commitments are quite similar. These actions can be seen in the individual as well as interactions with others in the organization. The consequences of a leader are a pattern of results. These results are impressive, and are used as a foundation for preparing the team and organization for future results and success.

5.

Understanding Foundational Leadership

Leaders are the source of an organization achieving significant results and creating value

A business exists to create value. A key element to creating value is to reliably and predictably deliver results. Further value is created when businesses achieve results beyond what is expected and what competitors are achieving. This calls for foundational leadership. That is, organizations achieve unexpected results, or that which was otherwise not going to occur, because of foundational leadership.

Leadership intervenes when the desired level or type of results will not occur absent some disruptions.

Foundational Leaders create clarity of purpose, appreciation of shared values and an articulation of the future that engages and enables those in the organization to take actions that will lead to results.

Intervention that produces the results is evidence that effective leaders are present. Disrupting the status quo to improve performance is a leadership role.

Definitions of Leadership

We all know, of course, that there are many qualities and characteristics of powerful leaders in an organization. When executives and managers are focusing on a specific discontinuous change - something big enough to actually transform organizations - there are particular aspects of leadership that must come fore and center in the being and acting of leaders.

I find that getting clarity on the definition of a word is a good place for me to start in developing a deeper understanding, and ultimately a distinction, in a field. This is certainly the case with leadership, and the kind of leadership that is required for strategic execution and transformation. Let's look at the *Oxford Dictionary* definition[4]:

> lead1 /li;d/v. *(past and past part. led /lEd/)*
> *1. cause (a person) to go with one by drawing them along. Show (someone) the way to a destination by preceding or accompanying them*
> *2. (usu. lead to) be a route or means of access to a particular place. Culminate or result in. (lead someone to/to do something) be someone's reason or motive for*
> *3. to lead people to have or experience (particular way of life)*

I would like to look at these definitions with you, and see what we can pull apart that will tell us more about leaders.

---

[4] *Oxford Compact Dictionary*

Energy

The first word in the first definition gives us insight into leadership: a leader is "*cause*." The leader is the cause or energy source of the strategic execution. Strategic execution and transformation begins with leaders. To look at this further, the definition of *cause* is: a "person or thing that gives rise to an action, phenomenon or condition. Reasonable grounds for a belief or action." When we look at the definition of *cause*, we first see that it is "a person or thing that gives rise to an action, phenomenon or condition." An intentional leader gives rise to actions.

If we look further, we see that this "rise" is not only an action, but also a phenomenon. Phenomenon is defined as a fact or situation that is observed to exist or happen, especially whose cause was not easily anticipated. Successful strategic execution is certainly a phenomenon, as it is not easily anticipated. In fact, the phenomenon of strategic execution occurs only through the intention and actions of leaders.

I particularly like that in the definition of *cause,* the word "condition" is used. What is transformed is the *condition* of the organization. The *condition* is changed so as to allow dramatic improvements in business results. The intention of the leader is to change the conditions in the business so that execution can occur, which in turn will further alter/improve the conditions in the business.

Foundational Leaders on the Field

Leading by Example

Another element of leadership is that a leader causes a person (or organization) to go along with them *by preceding or accompanying them.* A leader must precede those in the organization in making changes. In other words, if a transformation is to occur, the leader must be intentional about involvement in that transformation. There is no hiding out for a leader in a transformation. Not only must the leader be involved in the change, but she or he must also do so in a public manner. How else can the leader "show the way to a destination by preceding or accompanying" the people in the organization?

Evokes Actions of Others

The second definition also gives us an insight into a leader's role in transforming a business organization. The definition reads: to lead someone to/to do something. Leadership is about getting people in the organization to *do something*. In fact, it is getting the people in the organization to do something new that will produce a significant result. In leading a transformation, the people must act to produce a significant result and change the essence of their work and the organization.

Foundational Leaders in Action

1. Leads by Example
2. Evokes Actions of Others
3. Gives Meaning to People Being at Work
4. Gives Context to the Organization
5. Communicates the Shared Values
6. Establishes Commitment as Cornerstone
7. Clarifies Purpose of Change for Organization
8. Focus on Results
9. Generates Whatever Is Required to Get Results
10. Intentional
11. Inspires Others to Achieve Results

Let's look at how the leader goes about getting the people in the organization to act; the definition continues, "be someone's reason or motive for." The leader is someone's *reason or motive for*. People in the organization will act, based on the leader's *being their reason and motive for* acting. For a person who has grown up in a company that has a command-and-control culture, it is unnatural to think about being a group of people's reason and motive for acting. It is much easier to give a command or make an order. What is required for managers who have grown up in a command-and-control company environment (and most have) to make this change is a transformation of themselves, personally. That leads us to the third definition.

Gives Meaning to People Being At Work

The third definition is, *"to lead people to have or experience (a particular way of life)"*. Organization culture is what gives employees a particular way of life at work. Changing organizational culture is creating a different, particular way of life at work, and clearly this happens only when a leader is involved. What kind of leadership, then, is the key ingredient in the transformation of an organization? Leadership *causes* transformation to happen. Leadership *leads people to do something*. Leadership is *reason or motive for*. Leadership results in accomplishments of people throughout the organization.

Gives Context to the Organization

Organizations achieve results that were otherwise not going to occur because of the being and actions of a leader. Leaders alter the "being" of their organizations, giving others a different experience of what it means to be at work. Leaders get their own being from their foundational commitments as well as the commitments that they have made in regards to the business.

A leader alters the context and changes the culture of the organization so that the people are able to create or generate for themselves. This is the biggest gift, allowing people to learn to "fish" for themselves. It is like the old saying, "Give a person a fish, they have a meal for the day; teach them to fish, and they have meals for a lifetime." The impact of a leader is not only teaching people to fish, but also creating the environment in which fishing flourishes.

Communicating the Shared Values

The shared values that are articulated and come to be appreciated by the people in the business come from the leader's commitments as well. The values say what we believe in as an organization, what is important to us, and in what ways we can be counted on. Values for a leader will always have a couple of elements; one is doing what we say we will do. The second is results, or as one leader told me "Results, Results, Results". It is not that leaders are not compassionate people who care about their employees' safety and well-being. Most do care quite deeply. In addition, they appreciate that employees' safety and well-being is intimately related to achieving excellent business results.

Establishing Commitment as the Cornerstone

Leaders have enormous commitment. This commitment is to the success of the organization. In turn, others express their own commitments, and over time, the commitment is the common link for those involved in strategic execution and transformation.

Clarifying of Purpose for Change for the Organization

Leaders create clarity of purpose, based on the results that are needed and promised for the organization. A leader interacts with others so they are reminded of the purpose, inspired to act and motivated to take the appropriate actions.

Focusing on Results

The leader's purpose is to assure that the results are achieved. This includes achieving the results using appropriate values and proper actions. If the results are not being accomplished, then the leader is not getting the job done. While that statement may seem harsh or judgmental, I invite you to think along with me as to what that statement makes available and possible to a person who is committed to being a leader. Focusing on results puts in stark relief the reason for being of a leader and is a measure that is most valuable.

Creating Whatever is Required to Get the Results

Creating is a key aspect of leadership. The leader generates what is required to have the organization or team get the results. When you watch a leader generating, it is evident that the person's commitment to the team and results is so strong that he/she will keep innovating and inventing until a workable solution is found. The person will not settle for mediocrity or a defeat. There is a strong tendency by some to give excuses when an organization or team fails to deliver the expected results and talk about the extenuating circumstances.

Even when the desired result is not achieved, the creative leader's position is that we simply ran out of time before we could find the winning solution. A leader churns ideas and alternative solutions over and over, looking for an approach that will inspire the team to action. A course of action that is likely to be successful. The question that the leader continues to ask is, "How can we best optimize the results, given that we own this situation and have access to a wide range of resources?" There is a commitment to get extraordinary results.

Inspiring Others to Achieve Results

During strategic execution, a leader gives rise to belief in needed actions and assists others in generating the needed actions. A leader assists the organization in achieving what was otherwise *not* going to happen. A leader accomplishes results through inspiring others to act. Without this kind of leadership, there is little chance that a transformation will be achieved. With this kind of leadership there is enormous possibility that the transformation will be achieved.

Consequences of a Leader in an Organization

The word *consequence* is defined as the "effect or result". When we look at the effect or result of a leader in a business organization, the first place we should look is business performance. That is, performance to deliver the specific, measurable outcomes for which the team and organization exists. The consequence of having a leader goes far beyond what may be initially apparent. These effects or results are lasting impacts that go beyond the tenure of the leader.

New Context

In basic terms, the result that an organization is achieving is determined in part by the context. If there is a desire to improve the performance, the context must be altered. If the context is not altered, there will likely not be an improvement in performance. As an example, in a client company there is a large manufacturing facility that has achieved extraordinary business results. The results were far beyond what was considered predictable, and to some, what was beyond possible. Nonetheless, they accomplished the extraordinary. Part of this accomplishment was teaching them to see context and notice the impact that context was creating.

Effective Communication

Communication is how the leader impacts and influences others. Leaders create an environment of open, honest and complete communication. Leaders often communicate even when employees do not like what is being said; that is, the leaders are dealing with challenging and difficult topics. Effective leadership communication can, from time to time, evoke a comment from employees like "TMI – too much information". While complaints like this may be heard, leaders know that they must over-communicate in general and about the difficult issues in particular.

The core component of leadership communication is listening. The quality of the leader's listening is directly related to the effectiveness of that leader as a communicator.

Upward communication from those in the organization is essential for effective communication, as well as, success in execution and transformation. The evidence of effective upward communication is the openness of individual employees voicing concerns.

Energized Organizations

Leaders energize their organizations. A leader creates energy through developing additional leaders on the teams and in the organization. Leadership is given to the people. The empowering, challenging, honoring, etc. remains with the people long after the accomplishment is achieved. They take it with them. It stays even after the leader moves on.

Improving Organizational Capabilities

Leaders improve their organizations. Leaders demonstrate what is needed for the organization or team to be successful, and instill in the people a sense of confidence that they can be successful in a variety of circumstances.

Those in the organization grow in terms of their understanding of the technical aspects of the work. They grow in terms of their appreciation of what will satisfy the customer and increase financial performance. People grow in terms of their self-confidence and resourcefulness, and in terms of their willingness to try something new to see if it improves performance. Teams and organizations improve their capability and capacity to perform the value-adding actions that will improve the overall performance. This leaves lasting impacts and impressions on the organization. Leaders leave organizations in much better shape than they found them.

Developing Additional Leaders

Leaders develop other leaders. A leader provides the source for the development of others in the organization. When a leader is around, people flourish. There is appreciation of the importance of bringing other people along. It is essential to a leader that he/she appreciates the importance of helping develop other people as leaders; a leader can only move as fast as he/she develops others.

Another part of this development is modeling what it looks like to be a leader, as well as, the actions that are needed from leaders. Leaders develop others through modeling and setting good examples.

Engaging Employees

Organizations create value by engaging employees to provide desirable goods and services to customers. The desirability of the goods and services is reflected in the customer paying an attractive amount, which in turn results in profitability and value for the business. While this is simple and straightforward in concept, it is quite another matter to achieve in practice. It requires leadership to engage and enroll employees in acting in a manner that creates value for customers, as well as, the organization.

Empowering Employees

The biggest gift the leader gives to the people is the capacity to generate possibility and translate that into meaningful action for themselves. This includes being able to see the current context and how that context is playing out. Being able to see the current context enables individuals to see what is missing and to look at inventing what would give a more powerful future than is currently available.

A Legacy of Leadership

Evidence that a leader has been present in an organization is that people talk about her/him long after they are gone. People remember sayings and actions. They are aware that being in contact with the leader touched their lives. They openly talk about how much they wish the leader were still there, and how much they learned from that leader. Even people who were not particularly the leader's admirers now talk about his courage and clarity of direction. An outstanding leader is remembered for not just the results, but also for the way he challenged the myths. This is not about his having been outrageous by most standards, but rather because he was focused and passionate.

Leaders create a legacy of leadership not only with their own accomplishments, but also with the accomplishment of those whom they bring into the organization. The legacy of good leadership is new leaders who exhibit an exceptional talent, leaders who are set up well for success.

Research Data

A recent article in the *McKinsey Quarterly*[5] provides useful research-based validation of the importance of a leader in intervening in the performance of a business. In this study, the authors concluded that "an organization is much more likely to improve its current performance and underlying health by using a combination of complementary practices, rather than any one of them alone". The authors conclude that there is a *base case* of practices which account for at

---

[5] Keith Leslie, Mark A Loch, and William Schaninger. "Managing Your Organization by the Evidence" The McKenzie Quarterly

least fifty percent of the success found in their data. These *base case* practices are:

1. Accountability – design organizational structures, create reporting relationships and develop evaluation systems that require people to take responsibility for the results.
2. Clear direction setting – the future is described as broad, stretching aspirations that are meaningful to employees.
3. Culture – a performance culture that emphasizes openness and trust among employees and creates an environment of challenge.

What Does NOT Make a Leader

Pretending

You may remember the line from an old rock song "Yes, I'm the great pretender". Pretending that someone is being a leader and providing leadership is a foolish act. Those working for the "pretend leader" usually see the situation for what it is long before the peers or the boss of the pretender.

A particularly unworkable form of pretending is denial. That is, ignoring the data and pretending that you do not see yourself as the pretender.

Another tip is if you find yourself talking about a leader's potential (unless they are young or new to the role), chances are you are dealing with a pretender. The concept of *potential* does not occur when describing a person or business that is producing good results.

Focusing on Personal Attributes

The unfruitful discussions about leadership often start with characteristics of the person:

- Our CEO should look like he/she just walked out of Hollywood casting (e.g., Geena Davis, George Hamilton, etc.).
- Our senior executives should all be MBA's from Harvard University, London Business School or INSEAD.
- Our CEO's must have done a tour of duty in our largest production facilities (e.g., plants, mills, mines, refineries, etc.).
- Our leaders must have a low golf handicap.
- An effective leader must have charisma, be a terrific presenter, etc.

While it is common to talk about personality and personal traits of a leader, it is of little value. Both practice and the research demonstrate a poor correlation between personal characteristics and a person's effectiveness as a leader.

Giving the Title

There has been an interesting increase in the use of the word *leader* in job descriptions and names of management teams in companies in the Western world. This is *our regional leadership team*…this is our *lead geologist*…she is our *group leader*. While the use of the title "leader" has increased, I see little evidence that the number of leaders or the effectiveness of leadership has actually increased. That is because being called a leader and being a leader are worlds apart.

Conclusion

Leadership is a key ingredient in success of strategic execution and transformation. Leadership *causes* transformation to happen. Leadership *leads people to do something*. Leadership is *reason*

Consequences of Foundational Leaders
- New Context
- Effective Organization
- Energized Organization
- Improved Organizational Capacity
- Developing Additional Leaders
- Engaged Employees
- Legacy of Leadership

or motive for. Leadership results in accomplishments of people throughout the organization. Leadership perpetuates the development of others as leaders.

6.

Execution Success Depends on Foundational Leaders

Strategic execution success depends on Foundational Leaders. No leaders, no success.

Plain and simple, it is that way. Chances are good you already know that. The question then is "If most of us know that, how come so many execution projects are launched with an insufficient level of leadership to be successful? This happens because:

- There is lack of clarity on what leadership in action actually is. (Hence my focus on Foundational Leadership.)
- The leadership capability of managers and supervisors is over-estimated.
- There is too much reliance on leadership being provided by managers rather than also developing Foundational Leaders within the front-line employees.

Foundational Leaders

The action of Foundational Leaders is the primary focus of this chapter. Leadership occurs in action, and there are predictable actions that will be seen by Foundational Leaders. These actions are what contribute to execution success.

The Importance of Leadership to Execution

I am often asked what makes strategic execution successful. I always reply "*leaders*". With my response I noticed that the person who asked the question usually has a blank look on his or her face, as if to say, "Duh, well of course". Too often there is an implicit assumption that a process or technology is the driver of success. It is if there is some magic elixir that is required for execution success. For me the answer is nope, no magic technology, process, or "lucky pills" … only leaders doing what it takes to guide and inspire their people to produce extraordinary results. Execution begins with leadership. No leaders no success in execution.

Leaders are the foundation on which successful execution is built. To use an analogy, they are the cornerstone around which everything else is constructed. Absent a solid foundation there is little reason to expect execution to be successful. An obvious analogy is building a house without a proper foundation. It is not a question of if there will be problems, but rather, only a matter of time until the problems occur. So it is with execution projects that do not have the proper Foundational Leadership.

> *Leaders are the cornerstone around which everything else is constructed. Absent a solid foundation there is little reason to expect execution to be successful.*

In addition to being the foundation, leaders also create a direction for others to follow, provide guidance on areas of action and inspire others to act in ways that produce extraordinary results. All of those aspects of leadership are essential for success.

Missing the Obvious

If success in execution being dependent of leadership is so straight forward, how come it is so often missed? Let me offer some of the most common reasons:

1. **Lack of clarity on what leadership in action actually is**

   Too often I find that there is poor understanding of what it takes to provide leadership in execution. Often it seems like naivety of the requirements. It reminds me of when I was running marathons. I would train for months prior to a race, and on several weekends prior to the race, run at least twenty miles. The strategy was to build conditioning and duration to be able to run for at least twenty six miles. Leading up to a race I would invariably meet someone who had decided within the last couple of weeks that they would run the race without really training. Most often that was a bad mistake. In a similar vein, thinking that someone can be a Foundational Leader in a strategic execution without intense preparation and skill is also a bad mistake.

2. **Over-estimating the leadership capability of manager and supervisors**

   Part of the naivety of what is required to lead an execution is over estimating the leadership capability of managers and supervisors. There is a sense that "they should do it". Whether they should do it or not has little bearing on whether they can and will do it. Rather than assuming they should do it, it is essential to make a stark assessment of who can and will do it. Let's look at an analogy using my running experience. Qualifying for the Boston Marathon is a big deal for a marathon runner. Qualifying is based on the speed with which you previously ran a marathon, with some adjustment for age. For me to have qualified, I would have had to run a sub 2:50 marathon. That means less than two hours and fifty minutes. Given my best time was 3:22, it was highly unlikely that I would ever qualify. To have any chance, I would have had to quit my job and end my marriage, to do nothing but focus on training. I was unwilling to make the sacrifices necessary to develop into that kind of runner. Likewise there are many managers, supervisors and employees who are unwilling to do what it would take to become a Foundational Leader. That is not a problem as long as you and they are clear about their choice.

3. **Too much reliance on leadership being provided "top down" by managers rather than also developing Foundational Leaders among the front-line employees**
Success in execution ultimately comes from the actions of the front-line workers. They are the ones who actually "put the ball across the goal line". Too often execution projects appear predicated on the managers will get the job done, which is simply not the case.

Let's then look at the kinds of actions you will see from Foundational Leaders. These are the actions that are essential for success in execution.

Actions of Foundational Leaders

Leaders inspire others to take action. Leaders inspire others to reach for goals and achieve results that would otherwise not have occurred. In looking at how leaders make this impact, the place to look is at their actions, behaviors and communications. Said simply, to look at what leaders do. We will start at the beginning of leadership, which I call *generating*.

Generating

Foundational Leaders create the vision, articulate a future, hold conversations with others that excite them about this future, and then engage them in becoming involved. For each of those steps to be successful, the Foundational Leaders must first create or generate the step. Foundational Leaders generate a vision for the business. They then articulate a compelling future, which they have to generate for themselves before they can describe it for others. A way of thinking about generating is that the Foundational Leaders go first through each of the steps in the execution. There are no shortcuts, or asking others to do something that the Foundational Leader has not already done. Foundational Leaders create whatever is needed given what colleagues are dealing with. Generation means that the person creates energy and intensity for self, and eventually for others. A creative leader is not dependent on others. A creative leader invents for others rather than being a drain on others. There is a pioneer quality about these leaders, where they have the spirit that conquered untamed lands and caused people to follow them even in uncertainty.

This raises an important question: What does it take to be creative? Invention and creativity are two hallmarks of an effective leader. The origin of this comes from a strong commitment to the business, and to the people working in the business. One of the secrets of leadership is being able and willing to create or generate the opening or space for the others in the organization. This is identifying the gap between the current way of being and what will be needed for success. At first the people in the organization can neither see nor have access to what is needed. The leader fills in the creativity, energy and intensity to demonstrate what is possible and needed for the others. The leader literally "creates the intellect, intensity, courage and momentum to get the team/organization moving. It is like priming a pump to get it flowing. Of course this requires significant energy and drive. Often leaders report that they feel quite fatigued as a result of doing so much of the generation for the group. At times it seems like a mother cat that is feeding a bunch of new kittens, where there is a constant demand for more. The difference is that this is with adults, and many of whom are highly educated and highly compensated. Unfortunately, they like many do not have what it takes or know what to do to generate an opening for action for a group to be outrageous and highly successful.

Clarity of Values

Foundational Leaders generate from their values. The values of leaders are reflected in the values of organizations. Leaders speak from their values. They respond from their values. Their emotions are shaped by the joy of seeing their values acted out in the organization, as well as the sadness when they discover their values are missing.

Perhaps the most crucial value for leaders in execution is integrity. For many, honesty is the first word that comes to mind in talking about integrity. However, it is more than that. It is being true to your word. There is absolute validity in what the leader says and does. By valid I mean reliable in that it happens as promised or predicted, and the action is highly consistent with the speaking.

Integrity is a characteristic of a leader. Integrity is one of the best gifts that a leader can give the organization. It creates confidence, comfort, and a desire for belonging by employees.

Integrity is one of the key levers leaders used in strategic execution. Early in the implementation, the leader will want to watch very closely for the slightest evidence of gaps or lapses in integrity. Often it is little things, and those involved will assert that the leader is being picky. However, the key to successful implementation is catching these little gaps and lapses early and putting a correction in place. When the team and organization comes to a point that it can self-correct gaps or breaches in integrity, the leader can be pleased as the change effort is heading in the right direction.

Lack of integrity will ultimately doom a leader's effectiveness in strategic execution. We frequently see the negative impact that high profile executives with a lack of integrity have on companies and their employees. Too often these executives who got the business in trouble get a nice package when departing, and yet leave customers, employees and shareholders stranded. While there are numerous high profile examples of the absence of integrity in business, I also assert the problems caused by lack of integrity of managers and employees is much bigger and the value destruction much larger than first meets the eye. I assert that lack of integrity always has unintended and undesirable consequences.

Challenging the Status Quo
Leaders are often asking "What have we not considered before? If we achieved that, what would then be available to us"? Challenging the status quo is among the greatest contributions that a leader can make to an organization. Often the people in the organization have lived with the circumstance and conditions for so long that they have limited openings or perspectives for radically different ways of doing things. A leader helps them bring increased creativity to their thinking about the circumstances as well as new opportunities for action.

The leader's challenging of the status quo is at first quite startling, if not frightening, to many in the organization. It is thinking the unthinkable and talking about ideas and options that would have previously been thought impossible, if not crazy. And yet, it is the key to unlocking a new future for the business. There are few who have trained themselves to be able and willing to allow a challenge of the status quo to exist in thinking for more than a fleeting moment. Yet the executive who can encourage conversations about the future to flourish is truly special for employees in the organization.

Instills Confidence

Leaders learn to trust their instincts. This includes trust about others as well as about one's self. Trust of self is crucial to being an effective leader. That includes readiness to trust one's instincts about a person or situation. I have observed that as leaders become more capable, they are more prone to act on an instinct rather than waiting to get "all the facts". In talking with very successful leaders about their own development, I often hear this comment about coming to trust one's gut or instinct. Further, these leaders will comment that some of their most painful experiences have come from not taking action based on trusting their instinct, and waiting for more data. The time spent waiting was often a crucial factor in a lost opportunity or postponed action.

While having confidence in one's instinct could, at first, seem contradictory to good leadership, it is not. Please note that having confidence in one's intuitions does not imply being impetuous or impulsive. That is not what I'm talking about. Rather it is being aware of an impression or observation that is forming about an individual, group of individuals, or a situation facing the business.

In the case of assessing key people in the organization, leaders come to have confidence in their assessments of others capability, energy, intensity and drive to do what is needed. Ironically the most important assessments about people involves values. That is, wondering if the person(s) share a similar set of values. This is important because a leader needs to identify and act on persons in key positions whose values are inconsistent or in conflict with those of the leader. A person with different values will send very confusing communications to the employees, and will in effect undermine the intent of the leader.

Trusting one's instincts about business situations is crucial, because the opportunity for action will continue to diminish over time.

Intensity

Another indication that leadership is present is the high level of intensity. There is energy and "heat" as employees work toward achieving their goal.

Leaders who are working on strategic execution teams create opportunities for people to contribute as well as put pressure on each member of the team to contribute her/his best to the work of the team. There is also a sense of healthy friction, as the team continues to challenge the approach to assure the best result is achieved.

An experienced leader can spot a team and/or organization where effective leadership is present. There is high energy, passion and spirit that are clearly observable. It is also quite contagious, as there is a desire to join in and be part of something that is happening. By contrast, a team that seems confused, lethargic or slow is usually reflective of the absence of leadership. The intensity that is missing is reflective of the direction, engagement and empowerment of others that is so essential to success.

Learning

Learning and leadership go together. Fresh ideas and experiences are the fuel for developing and sustaining leaders. Leaders are continually looking for new approaches and improved interventions to drive success in their organizations.

Leaders are seldom "born". Rather, they develop their skill through a lifetime of learning.

One of the great things about leadership is that it is a skill that one can never perfect. There is always a new challenge and learning opportunity. It could be said that leadership is like golf. There is always room for improvement. No mater how good you think you have become, or how long you have been in development as a leader, there is so much more to accomplish.

It is also interesting to note that most of the effective leaders I have met are very committed to quality education, and in fact are very concerned about the limitations or low quality of the US public school system. In fact, several have taken on trying to make improvements in the public school system as a challenge. At the same time when I talk with individuals who are passionate about improvements in education, they often talk at length about the need to improve leadership in public schools. That is, the great educators are a blend of teacher/coach/leader. The interesting challenges facing education is a systemic problem that will likely be solved only through courageous leadership in the face of very strong opposition.

Critical Thinking

Asking questions and criticality in thinking are key dynamics in leadership. It pushes one's own thinking, as well as the thinking of those around them. Often there is not much of an opening for innovation or improvement because there is little opening in thinking. What is taken for granted is blocking the ability to think creatively. Thinking creatively occurs through challenging the assumption on which the current thinking is based. That is, challenging oneself and others to explore what is fact vs. opinion, looking at assumptions based on opinion and interpretations that could actually be inaccurate or irrelevant.

Raising the level of thinking is one of the most important contributions leaders can make to an organization. This includes asking others to look at what others have accomplished or is possible and then challenging all of the assumptions that are in place. These assumptions serve as reasons for why the organization could not accomplish a similar result, even if competitors are already demonstrating it can be done.

Critical thinking by a team leader on a project also has a profound impact. As the leader continues to ask the team to identify assumptions that are masquerading as facts, it will become apparent that the team's view of the challenge is shaped by assumptions based on the past. Critical thinking of how to accomplish results in the future will open up team's thinking. What begins to occur is that the team notices that it has reasons why it cannot even think of accomplishing these results. As a team notices this, they can start to challenge themselves about all of their excuses.

Once a team can see how they stop themselves from thinking creatively, they can then start to work in a very different way. That is, they can challenge all of the good reasons for why performance cannot be improved or change instituted. Usually the toughest challenge a team faces is their own thinking in the matter. Once this obstacle is overcome, the group becomes quite resourceful in finding new ways to think about their part of the business. The task is to keep the challenging thinking open and vibrant for the team.

The shortage of leadership in many companies begins with a shortage of critical thinking. That is the inability or unwillingness to challenge assumptions imbedded in the thinking about one's own circumstances. The inability to think critically about a situation is what leads to complacency, limited creativity, repeated mistakes, and resignation.

Focus

Direction or providing focus is another key element of leadership. The role of the leader is to provide the energy to maintain the focus. At times this is very intense, as the leader must put significant amounts of energy and intellect to keep the team focused and moving, until the team reaches the point that it can do this for itself. In the earliest stages of the team and/or organizational development, the work is to get the team formed and working consistently with the expected outcomes.

The challenge of direction and focus is ongoing. Individuals and groups seem to go off course in implementing large-scale change. They "lose the plot". When the magnitude of results and level of change is high, it is common that the team will lose its focus.

I strongly recommend the development of a clear charter for each team as a tool of maintaining focus. The role of the leader is to see that the charter is developed, and that it is clear and concise. Among the points of focus is the metrics to be used to assure appropriate outcomes to be achieved. Beyond developing charters, the challenge is what the leader can do to increase the level of focus on those things that matter most. One step is to stay close enough to the work of the team that the leader can spot when the team is losing focus. This involves more than listening to what the team is saying, or waiting for the team to say that they have lost focus.

Often you will find that the team loses focus and is quite unaware. The team may be very active and hard at work, only not on those things that matter most. The role of the charter is to provide clear guidance and expectations to the team. However, the role of the leader is to spot when the team is off-course and refer them back to their charter. It is amazing how often teams will forget their charter and/or become confused. The confusion is usually reflected in the team changing the deliverables or the expected outcomes. Beyond that, focus is actually a reflection of a state of being alert and shaped by one's commitments. When an individual or team loses focus, they usually also lose sight of what they said they were focused on.

Communication

Communication is the tool of leadership. Leadership cannot occur absent communication. It is essential for leadership.

Effective communication directly addresses the questions and concerns of the listener. Too often, management communication is viewed as irrelevant by most of the employees in the organization. The irrelevancy comes from the perspective that "none of my questions were answered". Leaders, on the other hand, talk directly to the concerns and questions of the employees. In fact, leaders seem to have a "sixth sense" for understanding what matters most to employees.

My observation is that this talent for understanding what matters to employees comes from a deep appreciation for the impact that employees can and do have on the performance of the businesses. Many managers give lip service to the importance of employees and then do not behave/communicate consistent with their stated belief.

Effective communication is open, honest and complete. Everything that needs to be communicated is in fact communicated. Effective communication is both whole and complete.

Topics that are "off limits" are stated as such. That is,

> *"I know you are interested in talking about X, but because of Y, I cannot talk with you about that today. I can commit that when Z happens and/or on Z date, I will be back to talk with you about that specific subject."*

If the "off limits" topics are cleanly identified and communicated, these topics will not be a distraction. If the off limits topics are not dealt with directly and cleanly, they will become a distraction to the listeners and fester with others. This may be used as an example of the lack of authenticity of the managers.

Effective leaders are continually looking to upgrade their communication skills. Most are skilled in using the formal communication channels. In addition, they build informal communication networks to get their messages out to the people as well as receive feedback on what is going on in the company. I will discuss this in more detail in the following chapter.

Experience

Seasoned leaders find that their experience equips them to be more confident and effective. This experience equips them to be able to get a quicker read on what is going on in the business as the areas of opportunity and any threats that should be addressed. It is said that better judgment comes from experience. I suppose that is a reflection of how the person uses the experience. It is like the old saying that there is a big difference between having five years experience versus one year of experience fives times. The challenge is what is learned or acquired from experience.

I think the key to building experience is the insight that the person gains. That allows for crisp thinking, as well as identification of the dynamics that are present in the business and organization. The insights are often gained by the leader prior to the leader being able to articulately describe the phenomenon. That is, the leader can see or experience something before they can describe it to others. Often I hear good leaders struggling to label or identify the insight or distinction that they have. They find this frustrating as they want to be able to pass the insight or distinction along to others. The frustration builds if the person to whom they are attempting to pass the learning is not patient with the lack of clarity and crispness in the speaking.

Action Oriented

Velocity in action is a hallmark of effective leaders. The leader's passions are manifested in action of others and self. Often leaders use the effectiveness and velocity of others' actions as a prime indicator of their own effectiveness as a leader. Leaders control their tendency to blame others and make excuses for non-action in others, and see the inaction as evidence of something that is missing in their own actions as a leader. This insight is the hallmark of truly effective leaders.

Leaders are impatient with delays and excuses. Often there is a complaint that the leader is being intolerant or unreasonable. To many that complaint would be heard as a criticism, but to effective leaders it is a compliment. Not buying into excuses and good reasons is a key to effective leadership in execution, as it avoids being stopped by excuses. That is not to say that a leader is a tyrant. What it is saying is that a leader is resourceful in inspiring others to work with the inevitable

Actions of Leading
1. Generating
2. Clarity of Values
3. Challenging the Status Quo
4. Instills Confidence
5. Intensity
6. Learning
7. Critical Thinking
8. Focus
9. Communication
10. Learn from Experience
11. Action Oriented

problems and surprises that occur in execution to find an even better solution, rather than stopping.

The action orientation of leaders is also seen in the mood of the organization they are working with. This can be a team, a project or an organization. When a leader becomes involved, the mood and intensity change. There is anticipation that something special is going to happen. There is a sense of confidence, a spirit in the team meetings and informal gatherings. There is movement by people on issues that have previously persisted or been allowed to linger. When watched from afar, or with a different perspective, it is possible to watch the action unfolding and heading directly toward a result. It is this movement and velocity that points to the presence of leadership.

> *Lee Iacocca is a well known business executive and writer. Iacocca initially gained fame because of the results achieved as CEO of Chrysler Corporation. He then gained additional fame with his book **Iacocca: An Autobiography**, which was his account of what happened at Chrysler during its remarkable turnaround during US automotive collapse of the 1980s. He was recently written a book entitled **Where Have All The Leaders Gone**?[6]*

> *Lee Iacocca is considered one of the iconoclastic business leaders of that period. What many of you may not know was that prior to going to Chrysler, Iacocca was an executive at Ford Motor Company. One of his accomplishments there was the Mustang. The Mustang was among the most successful new car launches in US automotive history. While working with Ford, I had the opportunity to talk with a number of people*

---

[6] Lee Iacocca. Where Have All the Leaders Gone? New York. Scribner, a division of Simon & Schuster. 2007

who had been part of the team that designed and launched the original Mustang. For many it was the highlight of their career. I often had the experience in listening to them that I was listening to a person reliving their experience of being an athlete that was on a championship athletic team. It reminded me of the play Championship Season, *in which the coach and players relived the remarkable accomplishments of their final season of basketball in which they had won the state championship. In the play, the actors recreated their experience and in the telling of the story, the audience could hear that they used that* Championship Season *as the experience against which many of their other experiences were measured. The guys who had worked on the Mustang project with Iacocca were very similar. They described how different that experience was from many others that they had at work and in their personal lives. As I listened to them, it became apparent to me that Lee Iacocca had built a leadership team on that project that permeated leadership throughout the project. For the participants there was a unique experience of participating on a team with powerful leadership being provided. That is what leadership in execution looks like. It looks like a remarkable accomplishment being achieved by a team of people who are inspired by their leaders.*

Conclusion

Strategic execution is dependent of Foundational Leadership. It is that plain and simple. Foundational Leaders inspire others to act in a way that produces extraordinary results. Extraordinary business results are what strategic execution is intended to achieve. However, the best laid execution plans will fail without leadership. No leaders, no success in execution.

Foundational Leaders

7.

Becoming a Foundational Leader

Foundational Leaders inspire others to take actions that achieve extraordinary performance. This inspiration occurs through the actions, listening and speaking of the leaders. Inspiration by leaders is how strategic execution/transformation is achieved in a business. Strategic execution begins with transforming how work occurs for others in the business, and given this changed context, employees act, talk and think in different ways. These different ways of acting, talking and thinking lead to extraordinary levels of business results. In addition, the strategy and transformation can be built upon and sustained since it is based on the people of the organization. I am focusing on what it takes to be a Foundational Leader. The particular focus is on you as a leader producing a transformation so that strategic execution will be successful.

Foundational Leaders in Action

In appreciating foundational leadership, I think the place to begin is by asking, "What does it look like when foundational leadership is happening?" I suggest that we consider that foundational leadership looks very different if you are in the midst of it verses being an onlooker. An analogy is that a football game looks completely different if you are playing in the game than if you are a spectator in the stands.

Let's start by looking at what happens if you are in the game. I have said that "scoring" comes from inspiring others to take actions that produce business results. On the field where the game is occurring, what does inspiring others look like? If you are "in the game", the leader will occur for you as a person whom you admire and respect. You have come to trust this person's honesty. You accept this person as being committed and working to achieve a future for your organization that is desirable. In essence, you are willing to join this person in the actions that he or she proposes, or at least to have an authentic dialog about the appropriate actions to be taken. The Foundational Leader may be another member of your team, a team leader, a maintenance supervisor, a sales manager, an executive, etc. The role and title of the person matters little. What matters is that this leader is willing to hold him- or herself accountable to accomplishing something extraordinary that will benefit the business and the people in it.

If you are not part of the business, the act of foundational leadership may look uninspiring. It may well look like employees having very intense conversations and talking about aspects of their business that matter little to you. While you might expect that a leader is giving the inspirational speeches we see from coaches and political leaders in the movies, that is not likely to be occurring. What is inspirational to work teams would likely be too boring for inclusion in a

Hollywood movie. It is also important to remember that what matters is what the people around the leader are doing, not what the leader is doing. Let's look more at what it takes to inspire others.

Foundational leaders inspire others to take actions that achieve extraordinary performance.

When I use the term "inspire", I do not infer to an emotional outpouring or reaction. Inspired employees does not mean that individuals are floating around the workplace with sweetness and light. This is not a tent revival where people are standing and clapping. I use the term inspire to mean taking actions that they otherwise would not have taken to produce business results that otherwise would not have happened.

Distinguishing Inspiration

Inspiration is a word that we use often in common conversation to imply something that impacts performance so that what is observed is beyond the norm or out of the ordinary. We say that a team played an "inspired game". We say that we found a speech by our favorite political candidate to be "inspiring". We sometimes honor a former teacher by saying that they set a good example and inspired us to go on and do something that we otherwise would likely not have done.

In developing distinctions that you can use to deepen your knowledge and ability to apply, I recommend looking at the definitions of the words we use. If possible, I recommend that you go to an excellent dictionary, like the Oxford English

Dictionary[7]. Let's look at the definition of inspire. Inspire literally means to breathe or blow upon/into. Taken a bit further it means to breathe life into.

Inspiration = to breathe life into

It figuratively means "to infuse some thought or feeling into a person or group". Many of the early uses of inspire occur within a religious context. Christians believe that the Bible is the "inspired Word of God". By that they mean that God literally used the Holy Spirit to come to the writers of the books in the Bible to "breathe or blow into" the writers the words that God wanted his people to have. The Holy Spirit is often depicted as a wind, so that literally the words of God were breathed and blown into the writers so that they were inspired to write the words of God.

Over time we have come to use the words inspire and inspiration in our daily lives. Let's look at some examples. I think that opera performers are an excellent example. A great opera performance involves being moved by the music *and* taking on the essence of the character and feeling what the character is experiencing. Great opera performers literally breathe life into the roles. Likewise great actors breathe life into their roles they are playing.

These are examples of inspired performance. What we are more interested in is inspiration of others. To start this exploration, can you think of movies, live performances, sermons or speeches that you found inspirational? That is, ones where you found that you were impacted? To prime your thinking, think about:
- In the movie *Rocky*, when Rocky ran the steps in Philadelphia.
- JFK's memorable quote, "Ask not what your country can do for you but what you can do for your country".

---

[7] Oxford English Dictionary, Oxford University Press. 2004.

- A particular moving sermon that you can still remember years later.
- A speaker that seemed to be talking directly to you and who prompted you to make a decision or take an action.

As you think of times when you were inspired to take action, you may think of words like moved, encouraged, engaged, evoked and prompted. All of these terms occur for us as calling forward action. It is this calling forward action that is the secret to success for a Foundational Leader.

> *Foundational Leader = a leader breathing life into the organization that would not otherwise have been present*

When I speak about a leader inspiring others in the organization, I mean that a leader breathes life in the organization that would not otherwise have been there. People in the organization have unique feelings, paths for action and thoughts as a result of interacting with a leader. What makes it unique is that it would not have happened if the leader had not been present. The act of inspiring is to bring something into existence that gives openings for action to others in the organization. Hence, when you look for evidence of leadership it is wise to look at the people around the leader rather than at the specific actions of the leader.

Approaching Inspiration

We have established that Foundational Leaders inspire others around them to take actions that produce extraordinary results. Now we want to look at a range of options that leaders have for inspiring others. Consider the following approaches to inspiration:

- Asking great questions that open up thinking.
- Assuring comments:

- o Affirming confidence.
- o Giving encouragement that they are on the right track.
- Guiding to get you on the right track and avoid unnecessary pitfalls.
- Confronting / interrupting.
- Expanding horizons and views.
- Making resources available.
- Accompanying them during the most difficult times. This is walking along side of them, not doing it for them.
- Assisting with technical solutions that they could not otherwise have seen.

Making It Personal: Different Strokes for Different Folks

Different groups will require different approaches to inspiration. While that seems obvious, it is worth a further look. To give you some perspective on this, fill in your answers to the following questions about which groups of employees you find most easy to inspire and most difficult to inspire.

The key is to find ways to inspire groups of employees to go beyond what they have known in the past and beyond their comfort level. It involves inspiring them to ask themselves the hard questions, and to uncover the opportunities that lie in front of them.

A group of inspired employees may look like a group of underground miners exploring new approaches to make their work more productive and safer. It could mean employees working in a factory find subtle refinements for the equipment that result in higher quality and higher production speeds. It may also mean workers in a mill finding alternative sources of energy to reduce the operating costs. All of the employees may be inspired, and yet none would be featured on a TV show about leadership.

Inspiring employees implies a relationship. This is a relationship of respect and trust. Employees are not inspired by people that they do not respect and do not trust. They will not follow someone whom they do not believe to be capable and concerned about their safety and success.

Inspiring actions in others includes building in follow-through to sustain the accomplishment. That is, to produce results beyond what is given by current market conditions.

Creating and Inventing

When a leader is inspiring others it is because the actions have been created or invented for that particular moment in time. It is their freshness and originality that lead to inspiration. Notice the difference between creating

Inspiring Others
1. Make it Personal for Others
2. Creating and Inventing
3. Generate Others to Become Leaders
4. Being Present
5. Modeling Desired Mind Sets and Behaviors
6. Communication
7. Achieving Results
8. Keep on Learning and Leading

and inventing something in the moment to inspire people versus trying to talk people into taking actions that were tried before. Even if the actions were very successful in the past, they were sourced at a different point in time with different dynamics at play. What is different is that in the past it was created and invented, and now it is going to be done again. The gap between invented and reapplied will lead to different levels of inspiration and results.

It is hard for managers to appreciate that a solution from the past is not the best approach. Abraham Zaleznick describes this phenomenon in his class article

"Managers and Leaders: Are They Different?"[8] He says, "Managers embrace process, seek stability and control, and instinctively try to resolve problems quickly – sometimes before fully understanding a problem's significance. Leaders, in contrast, tolerate chaos and lack of structure and are willing to delay closure in order to understand the issues more fully."

What managers miss is that bringing a "historical solution" from the past to a work team is like bringing an old girlfriend home to meet your wife. There may be wonderful memories, but it will not inspire the desired actions in the moment. What matters is what happens now, and what is created and innovated at this moment in time to create the desired actions. There must be a freshness and uniqueness to the thinking and conversations if employees are going to be inspired to produce excellent results.

This element of creation and inspiration also explains why bringing in "best practices" often does not produce the desired result. By definition the "best practices" were done at a different point in time and in a different setting. If the best practice information is used as part of the creating and innovating, it can be helpful. Unfortunately, it is too often brought in as "the answer", and implicit in this communication is, "if you were smarter, you would have already thought of this". It is no wonder that attempts to implement best practices fall far short of expectations.

Enabling Others to Become Leaders

Leadership is like electricity. It must be generated continuously. It can be distributed over much distance, it brings power to the organization, and it cannot

---

[8] Abraham Zaleznik. "*Managers and Leaders: Are They Different*". Harvard Business Review. Originally published in 1977. Reprinted in HBR January 2004.

be stored. The leader's role is to continuously generate one's self, in order to give it away to others.

Generating means that leadership is created on a moment-to-moment basis by the leader. The challenge is how to learn to generate. It is not something that can be easily taught. While there are conversations and practices that can be used to support individuals in expanding their capacity to generate, it seems that it first must be discovered by the individual. It is a bit like teaching a child to ride a bike. Another can explain the concept of balance, and yet it does not take hold until the child discovers balance in his or her own way. To push that analogy a bit further, a child who is riding on a bike with training wheels will get exercise and experience the thrill of riding a bike. However, the child will not actually invent balance for his- or herself until the training wheels are removed.

A leader comes to appreciate their role and importance it has on others. Being the leader of an organization or team is a special role that should not be taken lightly. Being a leader works only when others place confidence, respect and trust in the leader. If the leader's actions do not warrant continued confidence, respect and trust, the leader's effectiveness will soon diminish. Loss of confidence in a leader is hard if not impossible to overcome or repair.

Being present means emotional, mental and physical presence. It is hard to inspire people when they perceive you to be distracted and uninterested. Likewise it is difficult to inspire people when they do not perceive you to be around. If you are off doing other things that are more important, it sends a very strong signal about what really matters to you (hint: what is really important to you is something other than them and this part of the business). It is hard to create and inspire others without being present.

Alertness

Being alert gives you access to the opportunities to level the actions. It gives you access to areas in which the organization and teams may have stopped. It allows you to see the enormous commitment that employees have that is not being tapped. Being alert provides the opportunity for others to respond to you in a manner that lets you be a Foundational Leader.

What then is required to be alert? Consider the following:

- **Commitment**

  It begins with a commitment to stay alert and looking for additional opportunities. There are always conflicting priorities and demands on energy and time. Nonetheless the commitment must be greater than the circumstances.

- **Awareness of your impact on others**

  Experienced leaders have the experience and knowledge of what happens when they are present. The unexpected and unexplainable occurs, and often simply because the leader was being present. With the leader's contribution of being present, employees will make enormous accomplishments.

- **Energy**

  Remaining alert requires a burst of energy to get started. Once it is underway, the interactions with the employees will further encourage and source the leader. The challenge is getting started. Leaders often talk about the huge energy challenge, and wonder if they have the energy to create what is needed.

- **Freshness every day**

  A leader creates and innovates from the future to which he or she is committed that the organization will achieve. This commitment is what provides the freshness that is the key to inspiring others. When leaders fall back into speaking from the past, they quickly become stale and lose their strength to inspire others. In some ways it is like being an actor in a play. Each scene has to be created anew to be fresh. If the actor attempts to mimic what was done the night or week before, the impact on the audience is notable. Likewise in an opera; there are many people with magnificent voices who do not excel in performing operas. Great opera performers convey a feeling of the part as they act and sing. Likewise, effective leaders bring freshness to each day as they create and invent what will inspire others.

- **Willing to be surprised and "go with the flow"**

  Unlike a performer who knows the lines and music, and then imbues passion into the part, a leader does not know what will happen on any given day. Leading a business is a request for surprises. Some good, and some not so good. However, if a leader is to be present and inspire others, there must be a willingness to be surprised and then "go with the flow" that comes from employees taking inspired actions. At times it feels like an actor or comedian doing improvisation, where there is little to no foreknowledge of the dialog or music that is to come. What is required is innovation, as it is all invented in the moment. This is a huge challenge for managers whose approach is to control everything, make it all predictable, and avoid surprises. While this approach may work in certain roles, it will not work in the role of a leader.

Foundational Leaders

Modeling Desired Mind Sets and Behavior

A leader needs to "walk the talk". If employees are expected to challenge everything, including well established practices and processes, the leader should demonstrate a willingness to engage in the same challenging thoughts and discussions. If the leader is not open to feedback and ideas from employees, what chance is there that the employees will take the change seriously?

A good example of foundational leadership is when someone has openly discussed that the past failures in business were not the fault of the employees, but of the managers. Rather, the closed facilities and mediocre stock performance was attributed to management. A transformational leader must be open to accepting the shortcomings of the past so that employees and management can move forward to achieve better results. This includes role modeling the desired mind-set of taking responsibility for what had happened in the past, even though he was not part of the company at the time. The leader is able to avoid the blame and finger-pointing that otherwise is predictable. It is very common in business for the managers to sit around in meetings and blame the employees and the union for the problems of the past. Of course, the employees sit around in the lunchroom and the union halls and blame the managers for the same problems.

It is essential that a leader not blame the past failures and mistakes on the employees. While this is a common practice, it is not role modeling the desired mindset and behavior. A leader must continue to reinforce that management is accountable for the quality of the results, that management cannot achieve anything without the active support of employees, and that together they can be much more successful than working apart or against each other. After this clarity on accountability, the leader should then make sure that the transformation is connected to business results in the minds of the employees. A transformation that is not connected to specific business results will soon turn into a corporate program and lose effectiveness.

Communication

It is through communication that leaders engage and inspire groups of people, who in turn engage and inspire others. To be successful in a transformation, employees need to be more engaged and committed than they were prior to beginning the transformation. This engagement will not occur if they do not consider the transformation to be personally meaningful and essential to the future success of the business. All of that occurs through communication. If there is one phrase that you should remember it is…

> *I cannot hear what you say because how you behave speaks so loudly….*

Being the communication is the best way to be seen as "walking the talk".

An important ingredient in communications is symbolic actions. The employees need to see desired behaviors from the leaders. Beyond that, there are certain actions that employees consider to be off-limits. Usually this involves some form of a "sacred cow". In engaging the employees, leaders can say "there are no sacred cows here … and if you find one, help me turn that sacred cow into hamburger meat".

Another act of leadership is getting out and meeting with many of the employees. This act alone is often a dramatic departure from past practices and demonstrates a commitment to the employees and to leading transformation.

Foundational Leaders

One of the keys to success in a transformation is confronting resistance and engaging commitment. The leader must begin by confronting the resistance of their team and finding ways for each person to authentically commit to being a leader in the transformation and standing for the business achieving the results. There is an old adage, "Sometimes it is easier to change people than to change people". The leader must confront when there are team members who are either not as capable as they need to be or are not committed. Usually the most difficult ones to address are the top team members who appear to be capable but not committed. Until this commitment is present or the person is no longer present on the top team, the transformation will be hampered.

Achieving Results

A Foundational Leader inspires results that are beyond what is expected and driven by the market. A leader inspires the unexpected and at times the "unexplainable" level of results. A leader makes something happen that was not going to happen. An organization with an effective leader changes the trajectory of performance, and achieves results beyond what is predicted.

A business exists to create value, and the only sustainable way to create value is to achieve results. A Foundational Leader is the source of an organization that is aspiring to achieve significant results and implement any change. A leader creates clarity of purpose, appreciation of shared values, and an articulation of the future that engages and enables those in the organization to take actions that will lead to results. Leaders create clarity of purpose based on the results that are needed and promised for the organization. Leaders get their own way of being from their foundational commitments, as well as from the commitments that they have made in regard to the business. The shared values that are articulated and come to be appreciated by the people in the business come from the leader's commitments as well. The values say what we believe in as an organization, what is important to us, and how we can be counted on. Values for a leader will always have a couple of elements. One is doing what we say we will do. The second is results, or as one leader told me, "Results, Results, Results". It is not that leaders are not compassionate people who care about their employee's safety and well-being. Most do care quite deeply. In addition they appreciate that employees' safety and well-being is intimately related to achieving excellent business results.

Keep on Learning and Leading: Your Job Is Never Done

Being a Foundational Leader is a long-term endeavor. There are no quick fixes or shortcuts to avoid the pain of learning through trial and error. There is not a "silver bullet" that I can give you.

> *Your job of learning to lead is never done.*

One reason your job is never done is that being a Foundational Leader implies and requires an unceasing thirst for learning. Each strategic execution is different, if for no other reason than the circumstances and the people are different. Each group of people requires subtle differences in how they are led, and the secret to success is the leader learning what will be required to inspire and motivate these people.

Your job is never done because you must remain vigilant about the motives of those on whom you are relying to also be Foundational Leaders. One of the main differences between Foundational Leaders and others is where they get their satisfaction. Many in business get their satisfaction from being in the limelight and getting the accolades for what they accomplished. They want the "goodies" for themselves. This type of person is not likely to inspire others to transform a business. A Foundational Leader gains deep satisfaction in seeing others in the limelight and has a willingness to put the needs of the organization before self-interests.

Foundational Leaders

Your job is never done since each group of employees is different and finding the best approach to inspiring them is a challenge. The challenge is in part that different groups of people have different standards for acceptance and credibility of a leader. They have different expectations and needs from a leader and ultimately respond differently to the actions of their leaders. The challenge for leaders is to discover what will inspire *this* group of people. Not only must leaders inspire *this* group of people, but they must inspire *this* group of people to act in a way to produce extraordinary results beyond what they would otherwise be more comfortable producing.

Learning to lead is a life-long journey. Learning to be a Foundational Leader is

Being a Foundational Leader is perhaps the most satisfying role that a person can play, as well as the most challenging

the "advanced course" in this life-long journey.

Conclusion

Foundational Leaders inspire others to take actions that achieve extraordinary performance. This inspiration occurs through the actions, listening and speaking of the leaders. Inspiration by leaders is how strategic execution/transformation is achieved in a business. Strategic execution begins with transforming how work occurs for others in the business, and given this changed context, these employees act, talk and think in different ways. These different ways of acting, talking and thinking lead to extraordinary levels of business results.

8.

Future Based

Foundational Leaders describe a future from which to see the options available for the business and to plan the execution.[9] This is a complete and whole future in which extraordinary results are achieved. It allows the Foundational Leaders to rise above the current constraints and problems to see what is possible for the business and the people. This view from the future allows the Foundational Leaders to communicate with the various stakeholders in order to engage them in execution that is much more successful than previously thought possible. This requires strategic thinking; otherwise the "future" that is described will be a solution for problems of today, rather than an invented future. Discipline in thinking is required.

---

[9] Charies F. Smith *"The Merlin Factor: Leadership and Strategic Intent"*, Business Strategy Review Volume 5, Spring 1994, Oxford University Press

Foundational Leaders

Future

Future is what pulls for success in execution. Future is what inspires people. It creates a context for what is to come, and provides new meaning to the events of life that are currently occurring or are likely to come. Future promotes change and inspired actions.

Future is essential for execution as it provides the desired end point for the strategic initiatives. Further, future should be the starting point in developing the strategic execution initiatives. Future provides a destination which is essential in giving directions to people. It motivates employees to act in a particular way since future is what sets the context in which your people are communicating and acting.

Articulating the future is the work of Foundational Leaders. You should not expect most of your employees and managers to see a future at first. The initial articulating must come from leaders. Future is initially articulated by leaders and then MUST be demonstrated in actions. That is, the leader's behavior and speaking is consistent with the future to which they are committed.

Checking to see if the leaders around the strategic execution are articulating a future and behaving consistent with it is the check point on future.

Future context is made explicit

The articulation of future should also make explicit the future for the business. This is a crucial first step in successful strategic execution. If the context is not changed as part of the planning for execution, the execution will face many more challenges and likely fail. Future context is what allows employees to see how they can be successful as well as how what is being executed can work out well.

Organizational context shapes how employees see the world around their work. It shapes how events coming toward them in the future occur. That is, if these events are perceived as a threat or opportunity. Further, context often shapes what is missed or not seen.

The organizational context manifests the employee's perception of the businesses' future. If your employees cannot see a future for the business even after the leaders have articulated one, look at the context. The employees' perceptions are shaped more by the organizational context than anything that they hear the managers saying. This is because context shapes behavior, and the employees have seen behaviors of managers and supervisors that appear to NOT lend credibility to the stated future.

Often execution projects fail because the context is either not clearly articulated by

> *"Little minds are tamed and subdued by misfortune, but great minds rise above them."*
> **Washington Irving**

leaders, or the old context has not been interrupted. Attempting to execute a new strategy inside of an old context is a recipe for frustration.

The context literally alters the meaning of what is being said. This is crucial in articulating future that is different from the past for a business, which is the point of a strategic execution. Therefore you want to choose words in articulating the future that vividly demonstrate a contextual change. I want you to consider how to articulate the future context so that employees see the strategic execution as natural and obvious. That is, the changes that will be made are seen as needed and the right thing to do.

Since context occurs in speaking, look at the unique meanings that may occur for your people. Words can take on unique meaning. Let me share some interesting examples:

> *The word scarab is a good example of the power of context. The same word (scarab) has radically different meaning given the context in which it is used. The term initially was used to describe a beetle, often referred to as a dung beetle. Perhaps the most famous is use of this beetle is in ancient Egypt, as excavations have found images of this beetle that suggests it was of prime importance in the funeral rituals of ancient Egypt. The same term has been used in very different contexts as the name of a Formula One race car, the name of a customer made automobile, the name of a Russian missile, and as the title of a comic book series. The point is that the same word can have very different meaning given the context in which it is used. As a sailor I have yet another application. Scarab is also the name of a large and obviously loud motor boat, referred to as a cigarette boat. While I as a sailor personally experience these boats as a direct ancestor of the dung beetle, the owners of these boats probably do not as they spend several hundred thousand dollars on these boats.*

In particular I want you to think about creating a context that improves the probability of your employees seeing the drivers and dynamics that need to be altered, so that they can see the actions to take. As an example, if a person becomes a member of a militia, it alters how that person thinks about themselves as well as their concerns. It becomes apparent that they are preparing for actions appropriate for a military group. What are the concerns that you want to see shaping your employees?

Future

Severing the past from the future created by the strategy is essential in executing a strategy. The conversations from the past are loaded and ready to roll out. All you have to do is mention strategy and executing a strategy and there is a history waiting to be told. The limitation of history

> *"Ask yourself this question: will this matter a year from now?"*
> **Richard Carlson**

and the past is that it has little if anything to do with the future, and specifically the future that is being created by the executed strategy.

In a subtle way, the leaders need to assure the employees that "we are leaving the past behind" without condemning the aspects of the past that they like or condoning the aspects of the past that they dislike. The secret is to provide directions for the journey, using outcomes as milestones for the journey as well as the destination. In executing a strategy you are bringing something into existence that has not existed before and you are making something happen that has never happened before. This calls for clear direction as to how we will make the journey. The directions want to be more on what we will do and less on how we will do it. You want to leave the how open for employees to determine.

Those leading the conversation should be mindful to watch for insertion of what is perceived to have worked in the past into the conversations and planning for the future. Often these past based ideas are dressed up to look like something new. Perhaps the best tip of the past based ideas being inserted into the future is the "weight" of the conversations. If the conversations become heavy and significant, that is an indication that an item from the past has entered into a conversation for the future. The heaviness is brought from the past. An item created from the future does not have the heaviness.

Leaving the present to fly back into the past was made possible in the Back to the Future movies by a homemade time machine. In the movie the character "Doc" invented this marvelous machine inside of his garage and placed the time machine inside a De Lorean sports car. Who can look at a De Lorean car today and not think about the movie? The question is how do you design your strategy back from the future is you do not have Doc's De Lorean? The answer is that you become an inventor. Just as "Doc" invented the time machine in his garage, you will invent your strategy inside your business. Doc did the inventing by himself, while you will do your inventing in collaboration with your colleagues. Trying to invent the strategy by yourself is a mistake. It can be accomplished only with the collaboration of others. In the movie there is special equipment that takes the car and riders back to the future. In business there is not magical equipment, but rather magical people. These are the people who are committed to leaving the past behind and inventing a future that is compelling. These remarkable people are willing to sever their relationship with the comforts of the past and design a future with you. This usually involves thinning out products and practices to which they are fond. Yet there is willingness to let these things go in order to have the business be successful.

Dealing with elements of the past is like thinning a forest. When the forester studies the different species of trees a determination is made of the kind of trees to be kept for further growth and development, and which trees are considered trash trees. Which trees are desirable and which are trash is determined by the intent of the forestry group, and of course the manufacturing facilities to which the wood will be sold. Sometimes it is not obvious to the observer.

Let me share a humorous example. I purchased oak trees to go in the front of my home. In Texas, oaks are beautiful trees and highly prized. The business from which I purchased the oak trees came and installed them on a Saturday. I was so proud of my new oak trees. The following week I was in Louisiana consulting with a forest products company. While driving through the woods with a forester I discovered that they consider oak trees to be trash tress, and were actively cutting down oak trees the size of the ones I had paid a "king's ransom" to have similar trees planted at my home only a few days before. It was a classic example of one man's trash is another man's treasure. What some employees consider to be the trash from the past will be the treasures for others. Hence it takes great skill to honor what is in the past without bringing it forward into the future during strategic execution.

Fashionable among corporate staff groups is the fine art of poking holes in strategies. It is as if they are all from Missouri and must be "shown" how the strategy will work. While this is understandable, you want to maintain a commitment to thinking from the future back to the present. The corporate bureaucrats will likely attempt to discourage you, as this way of thinking does not fit their "certainty" profiles.

> *"The mind that is anxious about future events is miserable."*
>
> **Seneca**

The challenge is that breakout strategies never fit the corporate certainty models. Who knows how many strategies that would have created large value for the company were halted because it did not fit the corporate profile. What is intriguing is that the corporate profile will be maintained even when the company is not creating the expected levels of value, and in some cases destroying value. This external reality does not dissuade the corporate staff from persisting. The corporate staffs are billow-like in their attacks on business strategies that do not seem logical and predictable. Unfortunately, many breakout strategies do not seem logical and predictable. Rather, some are quite counter intuitive. One could see the brilliance of the strategy only by standing in the business and looking at how to achieve the level of outcomes needed to gain competitive position. The market place view is often not available nor of interest to the corporate staff types.

Structure for Developing Future

1. Declare commitment.
2. Looking from the future, identify what is missing and essential for success in outcomes.
3. Grouping of the above statements into 4-6 major categories of missing and essential.
4. Begin forming initiatives around the categories.
5. Identify new metrics for these initiatives.
6. Identify conditions of satisfaction.
7. Identify the outcomes from the moment of success backward to the present.
8. Identify the major outcomes that are needed along the way as milestones.
9. Future.
10. The most difficult aspect of business strategy is "seeing the future".
11. In my approach the strategy is to achieve a future that you create. This includes:
    - The outcomes that are required for the business to be successful in the future;
    - The kind of company that is desired (the conditions of satisfaction); and
    - The new context that is required for success.

12. It is from this future that the present is ultimately evaluated.
13. The process begins with words that create the desired future as a subject for inquiry.
14. The articulation of the future will likely include some descriptive language as creative language.
15. The new context that was developed earlier in the strategic processes is used and being evaluated.
16. The ultimate question is, "Does this context give us a future consistent with our commitment?"
17. Outcomes that "ground" the new future are also developed.

Not Future

Let's look at examples of where those around strategic executions were neither articulating a future nor behaving consistently with that future. If you see some evidence of these behaviors in your own execution initiatives, it is worth stopping and checking on these actions in more depth.

1. **Be inspired or else!**

   People are not inspired by threats. Forced compliance is not the same as inspiration, and of course also produces very different actions and results. Ironically many managers feel compelled to describe a future cloaked in danger and threat. That is like wrapping a gift for your loved one in old used rags. Not only does it not enhance the gift, it is a waste of the rags as well. Old used rags seldom inspire us, and old threats and concerns do not either.

2. Let me inspire you with our glorious past

While the past should be honored, it has nothing to do with your future. There is trouble brewing if you see managers attempting to motivate employees by talking about the past and encouraging the employees to act so they can return to glory of the past. Further, many employees may have taken an oath to not get caught in any more of "management's good ideas". This is not a fertile field in which to grow a future that pulls for successful execution.

While the past is comfortable and much easier to talk about than the future, it will not work. This lack of success is in part because what is thought to be encouraging is anything but. Your past is in the past, and your future is in your future. While this may seem obvious, it is among the most common mistakes that I see on execution initiatives.

3. This time we are going to get it right!

This approach begins with "we had the right idea in the past but for some reason it failed." We are going to do it again but this time will be different". Rather than being assuring to employees, this approach sounds more like bewailing about "If only..." That is, we would have been successful on a past execution IF ONLY... Bewailing over the problems of the past is NOT an effective method of engaging employees in effective execution. Such behavior tends to bring up demons from the past as employees can remember their colleagues pining over the lost opportunity. This past based conversation by managers often contains an implied "If only" conversation. Invisible to the manager is usually an implied "If only they would have listened to me" or "I was right and it would have worked out if only they would have done it my way". Regardless of the merit of the claim, it has little power to inspire future actions by employees.

4. **"At my old company (or location) we did it this way and it really worked."**

   While the person is attempting to give assurance that the execution initiative is doable since he/she has seen something similar work in a previous job or place. While the intent may be honorable, these approaches seldom if ever work. One reason is that the employees may think that the results in the prior situation were not as successful as described. That is, not as rosy as the manager remembers.

What is needed is a future to which the leaders, managers and employees can become invested. This is a future that calls out for commitment, and the willingness to be bold and stand for something extraordinary. That is, something out of the ordinary for this business. Future creates life, the grim past kills it. Ironically, attempts to execute from a good past will do little to promote success. Only the future gives life and gives rise to inspired actions of others.

Conclusion

A created future is the basis. This future is one in which all the results are achieved and there are none of the problems associated with today that are more challenging than they sound. This requires thinking; otherwise the "future" that is described will be a solution for problems of today, rather than an invented future. Discipline in thinking is required.

Foundational Leaders

9.

Communication

The medium for engaging and inspiring others

If you are going to be a leader of strategic execution and transformation, you are also "signing up" to become a great communicator. That is because communication is the essence of leadership. Leaders can do little without communication. Communication is the act of imparting, conveying or exchanging ideas, feelings, knowledge, information, intent, and strategies which inspire others to act in ways they otherwise would not act. Their actions in turn will produce results that otherwise would not occur. Communication is core to successful strategic execution.

If communication is so important, how come so many managers are so mediocre at it? I think it is because communication is viewed as an "add-on to the real work of strategic execution". For many managers, it is "nice to do when we have time". It is viewed as optional rather than crucial to the task at hand. As a consequence, many prospective leaders inadvertently undermine their own effectiveness with unintended communications. While they think they are telling their employees how important they are to the success of the business, the message given to employees is the opposite. Because communication is treated as an afterthought rather than central to strategic execution, these managers unintentionally signal to their employees that they are not important and at the end of the day really do not matter … even when the words coming out of the manager's mouth are about how important they are.

Communication in Strategic Execution

Communication is to leaders like air is to the human body. It is critical for survival and success. Let's look at an analogy. The bodies of athletes in top condition process air very efficiently. Couch potatoes on the other hand have bodies that do not process air efficiently and therefore require their bodies to work much harder. Persons whose bodies cannot effectively process air are quickly limited in activities and have compromised health systems. The analogy follows: top quality leaders are effective in communications, while "couch potato managers" are often panting from trying to stay caught up. Those with compromised effectiveness in communication are seldom able to provide leadership at even the most basic levels.

Success in execution begins with a change in how the employees listen for the leader. As long as the listening is one of distrust and overt skepticism, communication and change are likely to be difficult. Communication is a two-way affair. It is the flow of information, etc. from one person to another. It is also the filter through which the second person hears and sees what is coming from the first person. Too often the focus is put entirely on getting the message right and using the proper words. Of equal importance is how the message is being received. The quality of the reception will have a greater impact on action than the quality of the message that is sent.

Since communication is a two-way affair, it is important to identify the implied biases and concerns that shape how the employees perceive those in management. That is, how open are the employees to hearing what the managers are saying? Do they have a perspective of respect and trust? Or do they have a perspective that management only is concerned about management and cares nothing about the people? I like to use the word jaundiced to describe this type of listening. In many businesses, jaundiced describes how people experience communication. In a physical sense, jaundice indicates a medical condition in which a person's body is not processing bile properly, and their skin turns a yellowish color. One of the symptoms of jaundice is "yellow vision", which means what the term says. (Ironically the occurrence of yellow vision as a medical condition is quite rare, yet it is used frequently as a literary allusion.)

The illusion of the yellow color has been applied to "yellow journalists" who are considered to be biased in their reporting. This distrust of what is being said and written also applies to the communications in business. Many employees view what they are told as being biased and inaccurate, if not overtly jaundiced. Such a listening for communications from managers will undermine the execution of even the best designed strategies.

Communication is Core Not a Chore

In too many cases, communication about the strategic execution can best be described as an afterthought. Communication is something that we do because we need to.

Let's use an analogy of communication being a chore or something we do because we need to. Let's use the very common activity of taking out the trash. I take the trash out once, maybe twice a week. Is it something that I am committed to? No. Does it make a difference in my effectiveness? No. Would I be happy if someone else did it for me? Yes. Do I feel empty or deprived on those trash days when I am away? No. Taking out the trash is something that I do. It is not an expression of me. There is no joy in taking out the trash; rather it is simply something to be done. It is a chore to be handled or managed. How much does communication in your company look like a chore to be handled or managed?

Communication is usually thought of as something to be done. It *is* a thing to be done. It is a way of reducing a potential problem. Seldom is it thought of as the core or essence of leadership.

Let's look at a couple of examples:

- When you see a young girl dance around simply because it is a sunny day and she is happy, what do you experience? I experience the joy that the young girl has with this moment. It is not a big deal, yet it is raw with authenticity and expression.

- What do you see when you see a young boy score a goal in football/soccer? There is often a blend of excitement and surprise. There is a sense that a group produced a sublime accomplishment.

What do you see when you see a supervisor talking with a group of employees? Do you see unbridled joy? How about raw authenticity and expression? How about excitement and surprise? Chances are that you see a chore, like someone taking out the trash.

Foundational Leaders

Assessing Effectiveness of Communication

As a leader of strategic execution, you will want to join in with others to assess the effectiveness of the communications about strategies and execution plans. Candor is essential in assessing communication, along with the lack of defensiveness.

I am providing you a series of questions to use for an assessment of your communications. If you have already started the execution, you can use these questions to evaluate the current effectiveness. If you have not started yet, use these questions to assess prior implementation projects as well as other attempts to create change with customers and within your business.

Communication Questions

1. How broad is your communication?
2. How credible are those who deliver it?
3. How clear are expectations made?
4. How effective is guidance?
5. Does your communication evoke action?
6. Is the evoked action inspired?
7. Does your communication evoke action amidst bad news or crises?
8. Do employees experience assurance from communications?
9. How inclusive is your communication?

These questions are presented again at the end of this chapter in the self study section. Feel free to use these questions to assess the effectiveness of your communication. I suggest you give a rating for each question. Try using a five point scale, where five is a good rating and one is a low rating.

1. How broad is your communication? Does it contain only messages?

We often have a mistaken impression that communication is one-way. That is, flowing from managers to employees and occurs when sounds and printed materials pass from a company representative to an employee or other stakeholder. Do your communication efforts involve intentional means of listening to employees? Is a safe area created for employees to be candid and honest? If your answer is yes, you receive a high rating (a five on the questionnaire at the end of this chapter).

Too often the term communication is used to denote sounds and printed materials flowing toward employees. If you stand back and think about it, that's silly. Yet many in business talk and think that way.

Let me give you a little provocation on this subject: do you think that every sound you hear is music? I know that those of you who have seen the musical *Stomp* have found that sounds you never thought possible are entertaining, but *Stomp* aside, do you hear every sound as music? When your neighbor's dog is barking in the middle of the night do you wake up and think "ah music"? Do you wake up and think "Is that Mozart that my neighbor's Beagle is singing (a.k.a. barking)"? Not likely your reaction.

Neither do employees hear "communication" in the sounds that come their way from some supervisor or manager who is pretending to communicate. Your neighbor's Beagle may be thinking a Mozart aria and yet to you it sounds like a dog barking at a cat. Too often your employees listen to communication coming from their managers in much the same manner as you listen to your neighbor's dog.

Foundational Leaders

2. How Credible Are Those who Deliver the Communication?

The credibility of those who deliver your communication is as important as the content of the message. If the credibility of the person(s) is in question, the value of the communication is at best compromised, and may in fact be counter-productive. The lack of credibility by the deliverer is a stronger communication than anything that they could say.

How often has this happened to you? A group of employees goes into a room to hear a presentation by a manager about some important event or happening in the business. While they sit there waiting, a conversation among the employees happens that makes it very clear that they have little regard for the person(s) who is about to speak or no confidence in what they will be told. The entire event is viewed as a charade and waste of time.

I vividly remember one occasion when a major reorganization was being announced along with the intention for an organizational culture change. This meeting was at a hotel ballroom with several hundred people in attendance. I was standing in the back of the room. During the presentation I noticed a couple of people grumbling to each other. After the session was over I asked them what they thought about the meeting and the message. One guy looked straight at me and said, "Mate, what's gonna change? You have got the same cast of characters running this ship and ain't nothing going to change."

"Mate, what's gonna change? You have got the same cast of characters running this ship and ain't nothing going to change."

As we discussed this further, the guys quickly looked at the new organizational structure and saw that the same managers were in place, albeit with slightly different roles. This group had been in place for some time and had lost much credibility with the employees. In fact, little that this group said was credible. (Note: little changed in this business until there was a notable change-out of managers – especially those who had lost the most credibility with the employees.)

3. How Clear Are Expectations Made?
Do your employees know what is expected of them as a result of the communication? Do they know what actions you would like them to take? Do they have a sense of how you want them to be with customers and at work? Often, that is not the case.

Let me give you an analogy: how often have you been driving and found yourself lost? You stop and ask for directions from a "local". What is the chance that you now know exactly what you are to do to find your desired location? It all depends on the clarity in the speaking of your" local expert". If the directions are clear, there are usually visible landmarks as well as clarity on the action you are to take. "Go to the second stop sign and turn left". Most of us can follow that, as opposed to your local expert saying "Well, geez ….. I think it's over yonder…"

Which type of "local expert" are you? Is your organization providing clear direction to a business that is in the midst of major change?

To make matters worse, managers are often told that they cannot discuss the details of the strategic execution until everything is approved by some higher authority. The concern is a valid one that key information not be leaked or disclosed that would compromise the business. In some cases there are regulatory or legal reasons for not communicating, and yet the communications do not improve once the limitations are raised. However, often this guidance is taken way too far. What happens is that communication is not given to those who need to have an idea of what is coming, and worse little thought is given to how and when communications can be started. That is, we give zero thought to what will be communicated until the "deal is done".

While management may have good justification for limited communication during "black out times", that is not to say that planning the communicating should not be at the heart of planning the strategic execution. To employees it seems apparent that management does not think of communications as the core of the work, rather as a chore to be done from time to time.

Just as neurons are essential to your functioning as a human, communication is to a business. While there are many individual cells or neurons, these cells constitute a system called the nervous systems which is essential to your functioning. While each are individual cells, something magical happens when they work together. So do the individuals in a business when they are communicated to and given directions. Fortunately, our bodies do a better job of communicating with our cells than we do in business when communicating with individual employees.

The direction provided should also "mark" the boundaries that are important in execution. To "mark" means to establish a limit or boundary, with immaterial things as well as territories. It tells the employees what is "in-bounds" as well what is "out of bounds". On a golf course, posts are used to "mark" what is out of bounds. These posts tell the golfer that there is some danger in this area, and to be very cautious in looking in that area for their ball. It says, "Caution this is out of bounds and not in the proper direction toward your destination". In medieval Germany the term "mark" was used to denote a pillar or post marking a boundary or position of land. These marks were made with a stone or group of stones, which were tangible guidance for the people. Likewise stones are used for marks on hiking trails, so that the hikers are provided with direction to their intended destination.

What types of markers are given to your employees? Are there clear directions? What is your rating for the clarity of direction provided in your communication?

4. How Effective Is Guidance Provided to Employees?

Communication is essential to employees knowing what is expected of them, how they are to act, and where the business is headed. Too often this guidance is taken for granted by managers. "We told them" is a familiar retort. Yet "telling them" does not assure that effective direction has been provided. Further, the "telling" may have not been all that clear in the first place, since it was hastily put together at the last minute.

Guidance could be thought of as telling how to do something. My father was quite skilled at things mechanical, while I posses the recessive gene that makes one non-mechanical. My dad would give me guidance on how to do something mechanical, e.g., working on the engine of the car. I am sure that to him the guidance was abundantly clear. However to me it was not clear. He had "communicated", but clear guidance was not received over where I was standing. So it is with leaders. The effectiveness of guidance provided in your communications is determined by the recipients. It is what they get and understand, not what you said.

> *Too often the guidance sounds like one manager talking to another, rather than being designed to be listened to by the employees.*

Since success in execution rests on the effectiveness of guidance that is heard or received by employees in communication, you would think that it is actively assessed. Yet that is not the case. You would also think that the preparation is thorough to reach the concerns and perspectives of the employees. That also is often not the case. Too often the guidance sounds like one manager talking to another, rather than being designed to be listened to by the employees. It is like physicians who use technical jargon and expects the listener to thoroughly understand what is being said, even though they have little exposure to medical terms. Usually the patients have little clue as to what the physician is describing. Often management communications are so filled with abbreviations, buzz words and technical, financial, legal, or management jargon that any guidance value is lost. Hence the importance of asking yourself, "Is guidance being heard; do our employees know what we are asking them to do; is our guidance thoroughly thought through from the perspective of the listener? Effective guidance comes from communication that is thorough and well-prepared.

5. Does Your Communication Evoke Action?

Action on the part of others is crucial. Effective communication is designed to evoke actions from others. One clue is to look at the requests that are made of employees in the communication. Is it clear? Is it something that the employee can do?

> *Evoking action by communication is not an accident. It is designed, purposeful and intentional.*

Evoking action is not an accident. It is designed, purposeful and intentional. Let me give you an example. If you want your son to mow the yard, how do you communicate that request? In most families, the request is simple and straight forward: "Please mow the lawn before Friday". That is a clear request. I request a specific action (mow the yard) within a specific time frame (before Friday). It is a clear request for action to be taken. Chances are that will evoke the desired actions (assuming this is not the first time you asked).

Now imagine with me that this was a corporate presentation, and how it might go: You would rent a meeting room at the local hotel and invite all the kids and parents in the neighborhood. You would open with a slide deck of at least 100 power point slides. The slides would include relevant benchmarking data from other families where the son mows the lawn. You would have a detailed process map that familiarizes your son on where the mower is located, ten different approaches to starting the mower, architectural guidance for making neat rows of cut grass, and end with an inspirational quote as to why your son will be a better person for mowing the lawn. Of course your son would stop listening to you or tune you out after the second slide. While the content of your presentation could be excellent, it did not:

1. Reach the intended audience (your son).
2. Tell your son what you wanted (I requested that the grass be mowed before Friday).
3. Enhance your credibility with your intended audience (your son).
4. Enhance your credibility with your intended audience's constituency group (the other kids in the neighborhood).

However, those who really do not matter (the other parents) will give you accolades for your excellent presentation. Even some will ask you if you can email them the slide deck so they can use it with their kids.

While this may seem like a silly example, can you see the parallels for much of the communication in companies? If not, try being less defensive and look around again. It is much too common an occurrence.

6. Is Inspired Action Coming from Your Communication?
Inspired action is a creative way to deliver the requested actions and results, and to do so in a manner that is inspirational to those involved. Look at the consequences of communications. Are the requests leading to inspired actions? Do you see inspired action occurring?

Allow me to share another family story about inspired action. This one is from my own family. When I was about four, my maternal grandmother died and my teenage aunt came to live with my parents and me. Both of my parents were in graduate school so money was tight. We lived in student housing near the campus, and there was a tall cedar bush in our backyard. This bush had many bag worms hanging from the limbs, which my mother disliked and wanted my dad to take action on. Following his military training, he delegated the duty to the troops (my teenage aunt and me).

After some negotiation with my aunt, he agreed to payment for pulling off the worms. Silly me would have gotten out there with a ladder and done the nasty job of pulling off the worms and their bags. My aunt was much more creative and inspired. She organized a "Cedar Party" and invited all her friends to come. She used the money that we were being paid by my dad to buy cokes and treats for her friends. She made a game out of an unpleasant chore, as she invented a contest to have teams see who could collect the greatest number of bag worms in order to win a prize. Needless to say the cedar tree was cleaned up and my aunt never had to touch a worm. That was inspired action on her part, and pleased my father as well.

Effective communication is designed to evoke actions from others.

Effective communication is designed to evoke actions from others. I find that a good place to look for requests for inspired action is safety. Assuming you work in a place where employee safety is important, what is the communication of commitment to safety and request for inspired actions? Are you seeing extraordinary safety performance? If not, look at what is being communicated and how it is being communicated. Is there a request to "Be safe, work safe and look out for the safety of those around you"?

7. Does Your Communication Evoke Actions in the Midst of Bad News or Crises?

A special time for communication that evokes action is when a business is in the midst of crises. Even through there is less time to develop the communication, being explicit in the requests of employees is critical.

Let me give you an analogy. "Jury-rigged" is a nautical term for a solution that is applied after breakage of an important piece of equipment. On a modern racing sailboat this is likely to be a torn sail, a broken piece of gear or a broken spinnaker pole. The innovativeness in finding a way to "jury-rig" in the face of a broken piece of equipment can be the secret to winning or losing a race. My first race was years ago. I had an excellent crew, and we were winning the local regatta. We won the first two races and had a big lead on our closest rival in the third race when an important piece of equipment broke. It was metal fatigue on a part that I never even thought to check. Fortunately the crew found a way to cleverly jury-rig the boom so that we could finish the race, which was the last race of the day. By the next morning I had located parts that we could use in the interim and race on the last day. We won first place only because of the crew's innovation to jury-rig the boat in the face of interesting challenges. Upon reflection, it was communication between the crew that allowed us to be successful. I was a complete novice at the time, and so could not give useful directions. Fortunately others were more capable and I did listen. What happens in your business when something unexpectedly bad happens? Is there quality communication? Is there the rapid response to provide the guidance and jury-rig so that people can receive effective communication even in difficult times?

What happens when there are nasty surprises in your business? It happens to all of us. What matters is the quality of reactions and responses. Does your communication provide guidance and make explicit requests of your employees so they can act capably and gain confidence as a consequence of the event? Too often, managers spend too much time playing the blame game and not nearly enough time inspiring actions from their employees.

Do you have a plan for crises communications to employees? Ironically most companies have well-developed crises communication plans that are intended for dealing with news media. Yet very few have thought about how to inform and engage employees. Ironically, a crisis is an excellent time for leadership to demonstrate values and engage employees. If you do not have such a plan, let me encourage you to put together a contingency plan now.

8. Do Employees Experience Assurance from Communications?

Marshalling your employees to act is one of the major challenges in business.

> *Getting people to act usually comes after they have learned that they can trust those in leadership. Trust follows assurance.*

Getting people to act usually comes after they have learned that they can trust those in leadership. Trust follows assurance. That is, people will trust once they have a sense of assurance about the people in whom they are considering placing their trust. Assurance is provided through the leaders identifying what needs to be considered, as well as listening to others' points of view. Leaders learn to lean on others around them for insights and broader perspectives. People come to have assurance when they see that their leaders are capable and resourceful.

In addition to capability, assurance is gained as a result of honesty in thinking and speech. It is ironic that people often are willing to accept liars as politicians, but not as team leaders and managers. If you are to reassure your employees, there needs to be a strong sense of credibility and integrity in the actions and speech of you and your leaders.

9. How Inclusive is Your Communication?

Miniscule numbers of employees are often involved in the communications about changes in the business. There seems to be a bottling up of communication and data that is done all in the name of maintaining proper boundaries for communication. Too often managers are so concerned with averting a misspeaking about a pending change that they do not communicate at all. While the managers may keep the lawyers happy, they are inadvertently sending a very strong message to the people in the organization. Not communicating is perhaps the strongest communication of all. What you are not saying speaks volumes.

> *Not communicating is perhaps the strongest communication of all. What you are not saying speaks volumes.*

While managers may ask their employees to "understand the constraints", they also need to communicate directly about what they can talk about. That is, be explicit about the boundaries of constraint. Also managers want to be explicit in saying the date they will be back to talk with the employees and give a full explanation as to what is occurring and what this means to the business. Employees will be understanding of the constraints on their managers *if* the managers come out directly and say, "On XX date I will be back to you, and we will discuss this in detail." What often happens is the manager does not make such a statement about constraints, does not promise to come back at a later date AND does not ever get back for a complete discussion of what is happening.

Effective communication is inclusive. Ineffective communication is exclusive. What happens in your business?

Improving Leadership Communication

The first step in improving leadership communication is making the commitment to do so. That is, being purposeful and intentional about communication as the core of leadership and strategic execution. If that awareness stays in the forefront, most leaders' communication effectiveness quickly improves.

> **Improving Leadership Communication**
> 1. Spirit in communication
> 2. Enlightened
> 3. Sharing the future
> 4. Enable broad participation of employees
> 5. Inclusive of all groups
> 6. Turn up the juice
> 7. Make the formal channels of communication effective
> 8. Tap into the informal communication networks
> 9. Render the rumor mill ineffective

1. Spirit in Communication

Your spirit must come through in your communications. What happens when you communicate full out? What happens if you do not constrain yourself, or settle for the mediocre in communications? What tepid is to cooking, mediocre is to communications. What often is missing in communications is the spirit and heart of the communication. Just as voice is in writing, spirit is in communications.

When powerful communication is occurring, you can feel the reverberations from the commitment of the speaker.

You know that when you read a favorite author you can hear them speaking when you read the writing, like they are talking to you or telling you a story. So it is in communications. There is a voice that is speaking through the communication. It is not like a voice descending from on high. It is not something that is aloft floating down to earth. Rather it is the heart of the earth speaking to you as the listener. When powerful communication is occurring, you can feel the reverberations from the commitment of the speaker. Have you been in a concert where there were large amplifiers and speakers? You could literally feel the impulses of the sound coming from the large speakers. Authentic communication is like that. Rather than the impulses being produced by large electric amplifiers, the impulses are created by one heart speaking to another. There is the sense of real people talking with real people, and magic comes from this connection. It is hard to describe what it looks like when a leader is speaking to a group of employees. These may be hourly shift workers, who are in dirty uniforms with grease on their faces and hands. Yet the intensity and honor of the communications is like angles that are descending from on high.

Communication is an honor between people. To have the proper spirit, it is not an after-thought. The gift in communication is the spirit that occurs between people, and inspires them. Spirit to evoke action is not something that is done after the fact, but rather it is in the gift of communication and honor between people.

2. Enlightened Communications

Enlightened communication is rigorously telling the truth to the best of your capability. Enlightened communication shines a new light on a subject and provides as much information and meaning as possible. People are inspired when leaders speak from their hearts and tell the truth. Ironically this is most evident in challenging and difficult times. Your employees want to know that you know what is going on, that you share their concerns and pain, and that you are talking authentically and directly with them.

> *Enlightened communication is rigorously telling the truth to the best of your capability. Enlightened communication shines a new light on a subject and provides as much information and meaning as possible.*

Enlightened communications always begin with honesty. The only constraint to your honesty should be the limitations of language. By that I mean your capacity with the language.

Enlightened communications evolve from telling the truth all the time. Let's look at what I am _not_ saying:

- What do we think they want to hear?
- Which version of the truth should we tell them?
- We will tell the truth when is it convenient.

You want your people to know they would hear a strident noise if you were telling anything less than the whole truth.

If you are restricted from talking about something because of legislative or regulatory reasons, you will say so directly and then will "fade to black" on the subject. You want to make it clear that you will not talk about something that is "off limits for now" rather than saying something that is misleading or intentionally inaccurate.

If you want to be enlightened in your communications, begin with being truthful and honorable toward yourself and your employees. Blinking is a bad thing. The word "blink" means to deceive and turn away. Further, in competitive situations one does not want to blink when face to face with one's competition. What happens in communication with a blink?

Those of us who are parents probably remember a time when we caught our kids lying, or at least trying to lie. One time I was flying to Mexico with my two young kids and one of my business partners. My kids were young, and were playing a card game called BS. It is essentially a game of bluff, where you try to lie your way to winning regardless of the cards that you have been dealt. My two kids were behind me in the plane playing the game with my business partner Mike King. I heard him laughing, and after the flight I asked him what was so funny. He told me that my son was not really able to lie, so when he needed to tell a lie, he would look out the window rather than looking at my business partner. That is worse than blinking. Yet it was a wonderful communication from my son. He had been raised to know that lying was a bad thing. From earliest days we had a deal. He could tell me anything he wanted as long as he did not lie to me.

What sort of a deal do you have with your employees? Do they think you would look out the window and give away the card game because you are not wired to lie? What would they say about you?

3. Sharing the Future

Your job as a leader is to articulate a future for the business, and then make that future available for your employees to see. That is how engagement of employees actually works. You describe a future, and then each employee chooses to join in with you in acting to build that future.

> *Your job as a leader is to create a future for the business, and then make that future available for your employees to see.*

While speaking about the future is a major role of managers, too often there is a discomfort in talking about the future. It is ironic that managers are more comfortable speaking about problems than they are the future. They can talk about challenges this week and this quarter with ease, and yet struggle when it comes to communicating about the future. Perhaps this is because the problems this week are tangible while our future is not. It is actually created and invented. The best way to speak about the future is from one's commitments, and one's heart.

Foundational Leaders

There is myth among managers that "buttering up a person" is a good way to gain favor and participation of employees. While butter is spectacular on popcorn at the movies, it is a miserable mistake in communications. Rather, you want to talk as directly about the future and the business as completely and openly as possible. Said another way, maximum candor and detail. I have a client who describes this as "getting it all on the table, blood gut and feathers". This analogy from bird hunting implies putting everything in the open for communication and inspection. It is making everything open for observation. There is a funny thing that happens with full and complete communications. While it is not always pretty, it is authentic and reaches people in a place that is appreciated.

Often I have spoken with managers prior to a talk or a communication session with a group of employees. The managers are jumpy because they were concerned with what the employees would think. My advice is always, tell them the truth as clearly and plainly as you know how. Do not add anger, condescension, fear, or any other emotion that is not authentic. Simply communicate as cleanly as you know how.

4. Enable Broad Participation of Employees
"Custer's Last Stand" is one of my favorite Bill Cosby comedy routines. Cosby starts off talking about how referees have the coin toss before a football game, and the team that wins the toss gets to choose whether to receive the kickoff or to defend a particular goal. Cosby imagines how history would have been different if each big event had started with a coin toss. In this routine, Custer calls heads and the coin ends up tails. The Indians win the coin toss, and then the referee tells Custer that he and his men must go down into the valley and wait until "all the Indians in the world ride down upon you".

How often do your employees feel like they are part of Custer's army who just saw the General lose the coin toss at the beginning of this battle? Do they feel like they are doomed in the upcoming clash? Do your employees think they can make a difference? OR do they feel like they will simply go down into the valley and wait for all the Indians in the world to ride down upon them? Do they see a chink in your management team's armor?

Doom and successful strategic execution do not mix. If your employees are to be enabled and contributing to your business, they need to feel able to contribute. When your employees feel like they are part of something special they will make incredible contributions.

5. Inclusive of All Groups of Employees

Overt inclusion in communication is what you are looking for. You want to make sure that no one is left out. You want to put a blanket of communication over all your employees and stakeholders, so there is a strong sense of being communicated with and engaged. Employees have enough moxie to know when their leaders are walking through the paces as opposed to being fired up about the future they are attempting to create. You want to make sure that each group of stakeholders is reached with intense and personal communication. It is important that no one is overlooked or left out.

6. Turn Up the Juice

"Kick it up a notch" is a common phrase used by the different chefs who have shows on the Food Network Channel. This expression means increasing the intensity of the flavor in the dish. You want this in your communications as well. Elevating the frequency and strength of your communications is essential. Too often employees receive only a fragment of the communications you intend for them to receive. They are not given access to the complete story nor the passion that is behind the story. Too often what the employees hear is only a part of the story, which has the tensile strength of a wet noodle. It is essential that your employees feel that they know what is happening and more, what is expected to happen going forward.

7. Make the Formal Channels of Communication More Effective
Each leader has a variety of formal communication channels that can be used. Some of the formal channels are newsletters, emails, web sites, blogs, articles in the local newspapers, media interviews, letters to employee's homes, memos to be posted in the offices and break rooms, town hall meetings, etc. Too often leaders develop favorite channels and use those to the exclusion of others. I suggest that you use all of the channels that are available to you since different employees will be best reached by different channels.

Trendy new restaurants often have a line of patrons waiting out the front door. That is a great sign for a new restaurant. It is even better news when that line of patrons continues for years after the initial opening. What makes a restaurant attractive? In some cases it is the extraordinary food. In other cases it is the fun atmosphere. I once asked a person, "What do you see in the Hard Rock Café?" The answer was that the food was ok, but that it was a hoot to see all the memorabilia on the walls.

This got me wondering: what are the parallels between formal communication channels and restaurants? In both cases we want passionate customers. Yet in both cases we have to continuously work to improve the quality of the offerings as well as maintaining a sense of freshness and uniqueness. I then started wondering what it is that attracts me to my favorite restaurants. In one case, it is the tables that are made from nickel; the table tops are dappled with various colors of nickel. I like these table tops because one of my clients is a large nickel producer, and I like to see their product used in this unique way. Beyond that one odd response, the rest of my favorite restaurants are a blend of décor suited to my preferences combined with very fresh and tasty foods. That is like communications, isn't it?

8. Tap into the Informal Communication Networks to Get Your Employees the Information that They Need and Want

Ignoble as it may seem, the informal communications network is actually the most important in a business. By informal, I mean the communication that happens between employees in the business. For example, many studies have found that the most effective communication for employees comes from their supervisors, or the person they report to in the organization. The formal and informal messages from supervisors exert more influence on employees than all the Chairman's messages ever recorded. A funny facial expression or snide comment from a supervisor tells employees more about what is going on with the business than anything that comes from the "big bosses".

I continue to marvel at companies who attempt to flood the formal communications channels with messages and yet ignore the informal communication channels. That is, supervisors are not given the information they need to communicate effectively. Usually they are not trained in effective communication. Often they are punished for communicating "the wrong thing", when they were never provided "the right thing".

If you want to see what is happening in your informal communications network, sit down and visit with your front-line supervisors. Can they describe the strategy of your business in simple terms that are clear and complete? Do they seem clear about their role in the strategy? Do they look forward to fulfilling their role in the execution? If so, great. Too often you will find that is not the case.

As one supervisor told me, "In our business the top managers use the mushroom approach to communications." I said, "Really, what's that?" He said, "Oh its simple, they keep us in the dark and every now and then throw ____ (fecal matter) on us."

Is your business using the mushroom approach to equip your supervisors and those influential people in your informal communications network? Research and years of practice have demonstrated that employees listen to their supervisors and colleagues as well as disregard what they hear from top executives. Where is the mystery in this?

9. Render the Rumor Mill Ineffective

As a leader, you will get the rumor mill you deserve. If the rumor mill is running rampant in your business, it is a clear indication to you that effective communications with employees are not occurring. Denial is not recommended when it comes to the rumor mill.

Let me give you an analogy about denial. Kilometers or "klicks" is how most of the world measures distance. In the US, the kilometers are shown on the interior of the speedometer, and yet most Americans have no ability to judge their speeds in anything other than miles per hour. I like driving in Europe since I really do not know how fast I am going there, but I think in miles per hour not kilometers. I assume someday I'll have to explain that to a Gendarme (French police officer), but for now it is a good excuse and I'm sticking with it.

Are you taking a similar denial approach to the rumor mill in your business? I may get away with playing stupid about my speeding in France, but it will not work for you and your communications in your organization.

When I hear denial about rumors, often the manager will say "I don't really understand that rumor or what it means". Implied in the statement is, "By the way, I'd really rather not know". Ignoring rumors is a big mistake.

> *Rumor mills exist when employees do not think that they are able to get factual and timely information through the formal and appropriate informal means. If the communications systems are not working, you can assume gossip and rumors will enter the fray.*

What is unfortunate about this is that gossip and rumors are not reliable and often are damaging to people. If you find the rumor mill is rampant in your business, you can pine away your time sitting in your office, or your can get out and be in communication with your colleagues and employees. Rumor mills lose their potency when communications are working. It could be said that businesses get the rumor mills they deserve. What does your business deserve?

10. Make Communications Personal

Communication cannot be delegated. A remote control works well for aircraft and unmanned subs under the sea, but it does not work for communications.

Communications cannot be delegated or done via remote control. I often watch with interest the response of employees to video messages from top executives. Usually there is mild interest, like curiosity but nothing that looks authentic. Perhaps the one exception to

> *Authenticity is essential in communications. It must come from you and be directed explicitly at those employees who are listening to you and whom you wish to impact.*

that is a CEO with whom I have worked for some time. This person does not have the physical appearance Hollywood would cast as a CEO. This person is tall and lanky. When he walks he lumbers along; he is nothing like a ballroom dancer. His demeanor is not that of a rascal, and in fact he is rather reserved. Yet he is authentic. He has developed a skill for looking right at a group of employees and speaking from his heart. He does not duck away from tough conversations, and instead seems to go straight into the difficult topics. He does not delegate the role of communicating to others. He does not hide behind his position or his schedule. Rather he communicates directly to his people. How about you?

11. Walk the Talk

Often missing are the actions of leaders being consistent with their communications. If you say one thing and do another, the game is lost. The most effective communication is a raw expression of commitment and enthusiasm followed up with actions. Too often communications are sanitized and "spun" so much that they lose any power. People are inspired by actions of their leaders more than what they are saying.

The validity of communications is ultimately determined by the congruence between actions and statements. If actions and statements are not very similar, the congruence is low. In this case the communications will be wasted. If the congruence is high, credibility of communications will build.

Conclusion

Communication is the essence of leadership. Leaders can do little without communication. Leadership communication is the act of imparting, conveying or exchanging ideas, feelings, knowledge, information, intent, and strategies which inspire others to act in ways they otherwise would not. Their actions in turn will produce results that otherwise would not occur. Leadership communication is core to successful strategic execution.

Foundational Leaders

Communication Self Study

1. Communication is the medium for engagement and inspiration of others.
2. Communication is at the core of success factors for strategic execution.
3. Since communication is at the core, it should be designed and planned for from the beginning of deliberations about strategic execution.
    a. Too often it is not, and is treated as an afterthought.
    b. Communication is core, not a chore.
4. Leaders are committed to being communicators, whether they like it our not.
5. Communication is a two-way affair. In many ways listening is more important than speaking.
6. Effective communication involves speaking to the listening of those with whom the communication is being shared. This requires identifying the constituency groups for whom the communication is being targeted, appreciating the concerns that these people have, and talking directly to the tough issues facing those people.
7. Effective communication changes the listening of the employees for those who are providing strategic execution leadership.
8. Indications of effective communication:
    a. Involves more than a simple message. It evokes a conversation.
    b. Credible people are the ones delivering the communication.
    c. Provides clear expectations and information to employees.
    d. Gives guidance to those involved.
    e. Evokes action.
    f. Inspires action.
    g. Evokes action in the face of bad news or crises.
    h. Is inclusive of all those involved, and when possible, all employees.
9. Ways to improve communication:
    a. Make sure the spirit of leadership is clearly expressed.

b. Enlighten others with the communications.

c. Articulate and share the future.

d. Enable broader participation of employees.

e. Be inclusive of all groups of employees, not just the favorite few.

f. "Turn up the juice."

g. Make formal communication channels more effective and relevant.

h. Tap into the informal communication networks among employees.

i. Render the rumor mill ineffective.

j. Make communications personal to your employees.

k. Assure leaders and managers are walking the talk.

Assessment

Please rate the current effectiveness of communications about strategy and execution plans in your organization. Use a five point scale

1. Does your organization use the term "communication" to mean the information or message that is being conveyed or sent?

   Never   1   2   3   4   5   Always

2. Does your communication plan involve intense listening to your employees?

   Never   1   2   3   4   5   Always

3. Are safe areas provided in which your employees can be candid and honest? (This can be anonymity, or in some other safe zone)

   Never   1   2   3   4   5   Always

4. How credible are those who deliver the communication?

   Not credible   1   2   3   4   5   Extremely credible

5. Does the perception of the communications by the employees invalidate the message?

        Always invalidates   1   2   3   4   5   Never invalidates

6. Does your communication provide clear statements of expectations for employees?

        Never clear   1   2   3   4   5   Always clear

7. Do your employees feel that they are getting "honest and straight" communications?

        Never   1   2   3   4   5   Always

8. Are there unnecessary constraints on what you are willing to tell your employees?

        Many unnecessary constraints   1   2   3   4   5   None at all

9. How effective are your communications in providing guidance to your employees?

        Not effective   1   2   3   4   5   Very effective

10. How well do employees know what is expected of them?

        Do not know at all   1   2   3   4   5   Know very well

11. Does the "guidance" you provide make sense to all the employees, not just the managers?

        Does not make sense to all   1   2   3   4   5   Makes sense to all

12. Does your communication evoke action by others?

        Never   1   2   3   4   5   Always

13. Does your communication take the form of a specific request?

> Never   1   2   3   4   5   Always

14. Does your communication inspire? Is it inspirational to your employees?

> Never   1   2   3   4   5   Always

15. Does your communication evoke action when something bad or unexpected happens?

> Never   1   2   3   4   5   Always

16. Does your organization have a plan for internal crises communication?

> No plan   1   2   3   4   5   Great plan

17. Do your employees experience assurance from the communications they receive?

> Never   1   2   3   4   5   Always

18. Does the spirit of leadership clearly shine through in the communications?

> Never   1   2   3   4   5   Always

19. Do your communications shine new light on the subject and provide as much information and meaning as possible?

> Never   1   2   3   4   5   Always

20. Are your communications based on telling the truth all the time?

> Never   1   2   3   4   5   Always

21. Can your employees hear and see the future in your communications?

> Never   1   2   3   4   5   Always

22. Do your communications make the future real for your people?

         Never   1   2   3   4   5   Always

23. Do your communications enable many employees to participate?

         Never   1   2   3   4   5   Always

24. Are your communications inclusive of all groups of employees?

         Not at all   1   2   3   4   5   Always inclusive

25. Is there a tendency to have favorite groups of employees with whom you communicate freely and frequently?

         Never   1   2   3   4   5   Always

26. Are there groups of employees who are often left out or at least the last to know?

         Often   1   2   3   4   5   Never

27. Does your communication "turn up the juice" on involvement, participation and responsibility?

         Never   1   2   3   4   5   Always

28. How effective are your formal communication channels? (You might try rating each one independently.)

         Not effective   1   2   3   4   5   Highly effective

29. How effectively do you tap into the informal communication networks?

         Not effectively   1   2   3   4   5   Very effectively

30. How credible is the rumor mill in your business?

           Not credible   1   2   3   4   5   Highly credible

31. Do your employees feel like the communication is addressed to them personally? Does it have that person-to-person feel?

           Impersonal   1   2   3   4   5   Highly credible

32. How well do the managers walk the talk? (What is the congruence between actions and what is communicated?)

           Low congruence   1   2   3   4   5   High congruence

Foundational Leaders

10.

Authenticity

Leaders are only as effective as they are authentic

Authenticity is "habitual truthfulness" that shines through the leader's actions. Leaders must be perceived as being "the real deal", or authentic, if they are to be effective in strategic execution. Personal authenticity is highly correlated with effectiveness as a leader of transformation. The converse of this is also valid as those who are not authentic are less successful as leaders of transformation.

Distinguishing Authenticity

Authenticity is best distinguished as "habitual truthfulness". To reach that conclusion let's look at the definition of the word "authentic". The Oxford Dictionary defines authentic as "of undisputed origin or veracity, genuine".

"Undisputed origin" is such a rich description of the authentic leader. People around the leader will say:

- This person is the "real deal.
- This person is "one of us". This is said even when that is not actually the case. Yet because of their authenticity the person is "adopted" as one of us.
- Values are clear and concise.
- We know what he/she stands for.
- We know exactly where he/she is coming from. (*Ironically the knowledge of what the person stands for or where they are coming from does not mean that those around the leader agree with the leader, or* "while we do not always like where they are coming from, we never doubt it".)

Each of these descriptions of knowing the leader's origins is a high compliment from employees. It indicates clarity of purpose, honesty and realness. All of these are essential attributes if employees are to be inspired by leaders.

Another part of the definition is veracity. Veracity in turn is defined as "conformity to facts, accuracy…" Conformity to the facts and accuracy are great descriptors of authenticity as demonstrated by a leader. It highlights the rigor with which the leader goes about gathering data as well as the quality of decisions that are likely to be made. The last half of the definition of veracity is "habitual truthfulness". This definition gets to the heart of what I have observed about successful leaders – habitual truthfulness.

An authentic leader places enormous value on the truth, both in hearing the truth and telling it to others. This person seeks out "the unvarnished truth". There is a strong desire to have the whole truth told. In the phrase used for swearing in witnesses in a court of law there is that classic phrase: "Do you promise to tell the truth, the whole truth and nothing but the truth…" This is the level of truthfulness that the authentic leader desires and practices. One executive has a colorful expression from bird hunting that is used to ask for the whole truth, "Let's get the whole story on the table… We want blood, guts and feathers". This same executive is a strong proponent of "habitual truthfulness" as a core value of his leadership and of the values he wants for his company.

A naïve question would be, "But doesn't everybody believe in conformity to facts, accuracy and habitual truthfulness?" Of course the answer is no, but a more piercing question is "how come?" Why do people who want to be successful as managers adopt practices that have them be perceived as inauthentic? Do they do that intentionally? My observation is that again the answer is no, they do not do it with "malice of forethought". Rather it happens slowly over time and in most cases managers are unaware of their own lack of authenticity, and are quite offended when it is pointed out.

Origins of Authenticity

Authenticity begins with, or is sourced by, "habitual truthfulness to self" or being true to one's self. It is said that the worst lie is self deception. Authentic leaders are rigorous in confronting the awful truth about situations in the business, the consequences of their behavior, and unintended consequences of their prior actions. Leaders are in continual development of their own authenticity.

Authenticity with Self

Authentic leaders practice habitual truthfulness to themselves! Authenticity "begins at home" with oneself. Habitual truthfulness or honesty with oneself is the starting place for developing leadership skills. Another way of saying this is,

"Knowing oneself is the door to understanding others." The classic expression of "To thy self be true" is at the heart of developing as a leader.

Another classic expression that demonstrates the importance of knowing oneself as the foundation for leading others is:

> The air to a bird,
> Water to a fish,
> Man to himself….

A person must come to authentically know herself/himself if they are to lead others. This is particularly important when the leadership involves a business making a transformation.

Authenticity is demonstrated by people being intensely honest with themselves about the condition of the business, the challenges facing the business, the competitive forces at play, the strengths of the management, capabilities of the organization, etc. The persons are equally as candid with themselves about themselves. There is no hiding from biases, blind spots, character flaws, strengths, temperament, tendencies, and weaknesses. Authenticity comes from habitual truthfulness to self about self and one's situation.

Continued Development of One's Authenticity

Effective leaders continue to develop and expand their level of authenticity. While authenticity is ingrained during childhood it must also be nurtured and developed as an adult. The motivation to develop effectiveness as a leader calls for a person to continue to develop their own authenticity. As a value, being authentic with self begins early in life. Successful leaders come with a value for authenticity that is started in their upbringing. In addition, successful leaders actively develop and mature their authenticity. The motivation for this development comes from their commitment to be effective as a leader. Said in other ways, at least some elements of authenticity are intentionally developed. The leader is intentional in developing and expanding their leadership effectiveness. Working to be as authentic as possible is a key element of this development.

In talking with effective leaders, I notice that they have been good students of their mentors. They have either patterned themselves after their mentor's strengths, or in some cases developed themselves in areas that they perceived to be a weakness of their mentors. One attribute that I have heard described about the mentors is that they were "present". "Present" is both a state of being as well as physical presence. As a state of being, the mentors are described as "here with me". In conversations, the mentors listened intently and then asked good questions. Another great gift a mentor gave to the leaders was demonstrating their commitment through paying close attention to the ones being mentored. Being present is then developed by authentic leaders. When employees are around them, the employees report that they had the experience of being present with a real leader. The authenticity of the leader's commitments supersedes whatever is said and is clearly communicated to the employees. Employees experience the genuineness of their leader. This is often described as this person is "the real deal". What can be more important than having employees think that their leader is genuine and real?

As leaders mature they come to appreciate the special power of being authentic. It is seen with great clarity, as is the lack of authenticity in others. I was working with a CEO who was an authentic leader. His direct report, who was a de facto COO, was an incredibly bright and talented person. He had impeccable credentials and was most adept in dealing with the Board. The problem was that when he was in groups of employees he came across as hollow and plastic. The

CEO was most concerned about this, as he knew that it would eventually lead to significant operational problems. The CEO tried to counsel the direct report on how to interact differently with employee groups. In retrospect, I can now see that the problem was that the COO was not authentic, and the employees knew it. The employees figured it out much sooner than the CEO or I.

Importance of Authenticity

Strategic execution depends on excellent leaders. In turn, this calls for authenticity in leaders at all levels of the business. Leaders must be perceived as being authentic if they are to be effective in strategic execution. Personal authenticity is highly correlated with effectiveness as leaders of transformation. Let's look at Chart 1 which illustrates the relationship of authenticity and results:

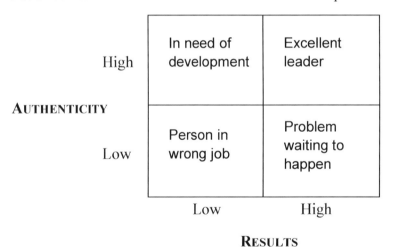

Chart 1 illustrates the relationship between authenticity and results

Authenticity in Action

Descriptions for Authenticity in Action:
- Acts responsibly
- Veracity
- Consistently authentic
- Authenticity in communications
- Makes personal changes as needed to improve as a leader
- Authentic desire for a better future
- Honors boundaries that matter to others
- Tolerant of mistakes
- Chaotic nature of transformation
- Knows what to say and what not to say
- Expands learning for all
- Avoids relying on excuses
- Accepts responsibility rather than blaming others
- Acknowledges facts and avoids using denial
- Avoids relying on excuses

Each of these will be discussed in some detail. However, please remember that it is the whole picture of authenticity created by these that is more important than any individual attribute.

Acts Responsibly

Leadership is demonstrated by initiating action. The actions that are consistent with the prior statements of intent by the leader are important to having the employees see that the leader is authentic, and that there is a path in which they can participate. The authenticity of leaders and employees pays off when there are actions that improve the relations and delivery to customers.

Acts responsibly is a hallmark of a successful leader. When I am with great leaders I am always struck with how responsible they are for themselves and others. Not only do they act responsibly, they are preoccupied with being responsible. That is, having their commitment to responsibility be clear and evident. This responsibility goes beyond the obvious being responsible for the business and the consequences of the actions taken. It applies to deep concern for families of employees, employees' health and well being, the impact the business is having on the community, etc.

Being responsible often occurs as being of service to others in the organization; for example, any number of times I have been flying with leaders on a corporate aircraft and observed that the leader was the one who was getting up to get food and drinks and making sure that everyone on board was comfortable. The same leaders are also quite concerned with making sure that the flight plan would assure safety over everything else. These leaders literally are "being responsible" for those around them.

Being responsible includes "owning" one's own authenticity, and on occasion, lack thereof. "Ownership" is of the personal characteristics, temperament and traits. A leader "owns" these aspects of self and "manages self". In contrast, managers who do not "own their characteristics" are often at the effect of them. When a manager is at the effect of personal characteristics they are not going to be successful in leading change.

One of my favorite examples is an executive who was responsible for his own misbehavior:

> *My partner and I were working with the president of the U.S. subsidiary of a European company. We were working on some particularly "knotty issues" at the request of the president. In our work we discovered that the president was actually the culprit, or the cause of much of the "knottiness". With appropriate deference we confronted the president about his behavior, and wondered what would be his response. The president listened intently, and then leaned back in his chair and said, "Well that is just one small smudge on a very dirty window". With that, it was clear to me that the President was aware of what he had done, and how the consequences had turned out to be different than he expected. Rather than blaming others or making the consultants wrong, he "owned" what he had done and the consequences.*

Veracity

The one attribute that cannot be in question for employees with their leaders is honesty. Authentic leaders can be counted on to tell the truth. They will tell the truth to the best of their abilities. They will avoid lying and misleading their people at all costs. They know that their integrity is key to their credibility and in turn to their effectiveness as leaders.

In contrast, managers whom have struggled with honesty are ultimately not effective as leaders. They may get away with it for a while, but employees eventually catch on and the person loses credibility. A loss of credibility with employees and managers becomes an irreconcilable problem at some point, at least in good companies. Frankly, in lousy or weak companies lying seems to thrive as long as the company survives.

The classic example of lack of veracity is a manager who makes a practice of saying what they think others want to hear. This usually begins as a technique for "managing up". Telling the boss what he wants to hear is an effective technique for getting along in many corporations. The drawback is that the manager soon develops a reputation for telling the boss and others what they want to hear and loses the respect of peers, direct reports and others in the business. These managers often become so skilled at saying what others want to hear, that they come to believe their "tales" as though there were the truth. In fact, these managers will often chastise direct reports for providing data and information that contradicts the "tale". The "tales" that were made up to satisfy a boss often turn into myths that are promoted throughout the business. Some classic examples are "Our customers prefer to do business with us rather than our competition, our products and services are better than our competitors; our costs are lower than our competitors, etc." These myths persist even when there is hard data to the contrary. There is always another explanation or story that supports the myth and invalidates the data.

Consistently Authentic

Consistency is a characteristic of authentic leaders. These leaders have consistently been authentic in each of their positions. When employees check out the manager's reputation with employees who worked with this person in the past, they hear very consistent reports of a manager who is authentic and effective as a leader.

It is a significant challenge when a manager who has a reputation for not being authentic attempts to guide a transformation. This person's past behavior is often described as inconsistent and at time suppressive. The person is also associated or linked with difficult times in the organization, and this person is "blamed" for negative events that occurred in the past. There is a reservation of employees to believe this person or to trust them to lead. Any sign of defensiveness on the part of the manager is viewed as more evidence that the person should not be trusted. In some ways, this manager is considered guilty until proven innocent.

Authenticity in Communications

Effective leaders are skilled at communication, and authenticity is a cornerstone of those communications. This is not to say that they are charismatic and gifted orators. No, many are not. However their authenticity shines through so brightly that any limitations with language are ignored.

A leader will say what needs to be heard, whether it is popular or not. Their communications are focused, direct and as "plain as possible". The desire is to speak to the heart of the matter so that genuine communications may occur. Even in challenging situations, an authentic leader is consistent and factual in describing the situation, the intent and the request for changes.

The authentic leader is highly consistent when meeting or talking with employees. The employees appreciate and are assured by the leader's consistency. Consistency should not be confused with condescending or telling employees what they want to hear. Often it is just the opposite, where the leader has a strong message that needs to be heard.

The authentic leader does not duck hard questions, but rather speaks directly to the hard questions and asks to get all of the hard questions out on the table. What is more elegant than someone who is plain spoken and talks directly to the point?

In contrast, managers who are not effective as leaders are often not authentic in their communications. Inauthenticity in communications includes misrepresenting and misleading employees. There is a long miserable past of managers communicating data and interpretations to employees with the intention of getting a compromise, change in work practices, more advantageous labor contracts, and/or wage concessions.

Other managers seem unable to be authentic in their communications. Often these managers are attempting to impress others with their education and intellect. Rather than talking directly and to the point, they go off on tangents filled with theory. They seem to practice the fine art of obfuscation, which assures that the employees do not fully appreciate or understand what is being communicated. What these managers do not appreciate is how much credibility they lose with the employees.

On occasion there is a desire to "pump up the troops", and so the manager will say things that are not factual and, in fact, may know not to be accurate. The excuse given is that "our team needed to hear positive things". It is like a coach of a sports team that is in the final minutes of a game and is trying to exhort the players to give the final bit of energy in hopes of winning the game. "You look great", "You can do it", "You've got them where you want them", etc. are all typical comments from coaches. Of course, for the fatigued players, that probably is better than "You look like a dirty dish rag," "Your incompetence is amazing," "This game is so lost that I do not know why I stay here watching you", etc. Yet, business teams are seldom in the final minutes of a game in which "white lies" are appropriate. Yet, there are many managers who justify saying "good things" that simply are inaccurate. The predicament is that these managers often come to believe the "white lies" they have told to the troops, i.e., the white lies become their reality.

Makes Personal Changes as Needed to Improve as a Leader

Authentic leaders are passionate about learning how to be more authentic and effective as a leader. They are committed to their own personal development. A leader must be willing to make personal changes as part of providing leadership for a business in midst of transformation. The leader gets to go first in personal change. The leader must be "in the game of transformation", and "being in the game" invariably means discovering things about oneself that will need to be altered or changed as the business transforms. Authentic leaders push on through developing self and making changes as needed. Inauthentic managers do not. In fact, I would say that managers who are unwilling to deal with their own developmental issues are one of the biggest factors in failed or sub-optimized transformation efforts.

Being authentic with oneself is essential for growth and change. Being authentic or practicing "habitual truthfulness" gives the leader an accurate reading on where to start in their personal changes. That is, more awareness of what needs to be worked on and developed. Changing oneself does not always come through formal coaching or coursework, although in most cases that is helpful. Usually the authentic executive is a very good student in learning about how to be a better leader and how to engage and inspire others to be involved in changing the business.

A leader's knowledge of self combined with continual learning also serves to guide the leader during the challenging periods of a transformation. This guiding mechanism is for the leader as a person as well as the organization. The leader is continuously looking to develop the skills that will be required for success.

Let me provide a rich example of this. My father was a reluctant soldier in World War II. He was drafted, and after completing the various training, was sent to

Europe. He was a young officer who was assigned to lead platoons on the front-lines in France against the German army. One skill that he realized that he needed was to know where he was located, especially on night patrols. This was long before the days of GPS, and so the key instrument was a compass. However, it was dangerous to look at a compass at night because of the light. My dad taught himself to always know which way was north, which would allow him to have a good estimate of his location. This was a leadership skill that he developed to protect his men and himself. In less dramatic ways, leaders develop skills from continuously learning, enabling them to provide better leadership to their organization.

Just as a leader is always a work in progress, no two strategic executions or transformations are the same. What worked for a leader in one transformation may not work at all in the second one. It is this challenge to adapt and continuously learn that makes leading a transformation so special.

As previously mentioned, managers who are unwilling to deal with their own developmental issues are one of the biggest factors in failed or sub-optimized transformation efforts. I have seen very different results from the decisions made by two managers facing similar personal challenges and provided with the same developmental opportunity. One was eagerly engaged with the opportunity. The term eager should not be interpreted as each day was a piece of cake. It was not. Personal development in the areas of one's authenticity is uncomfortable, if not down right scary. There are many feelings that are aroused, and invariably one's personal history gets revealed. An authentic leader views this as part of the price to be paid in developing the capacity to lead more effectively in ever increasing business environments. By the way, in case you are thinking that this person must be a soft, touchy feely type, let me assure you that you are far from the truth. This person is a strong, tough operator whose commitments are bigger than the fear.

A second manager was given the same coaching and developmental opportunities. This person voiced their strong commitment to leading transformation in the organization. This person said all the right things and appeared to be doing the right things until that fateful day when it became apparent that personal changes would be needed. At that point the manager simply stopped. The manager withdrew from active developmental coaching and began "pulling the plug" on transformation. The transformation effort was quietly shifted to an internal continuous improvement program, which assured that it would not require any personal development by the manager.

Other managers are craftier in how they avoid personal development. Some of my favorite methods for crafty avoidance are:

- "I'm all for you guys creating a transformation and increasing the value of this business, but do not expect me to be involved."
- "I'll stand on the sideline and watch." (The implied message is: "If it works out, I'll take the credit, and if it does not work out, you'll take the blame.")
- "I'm too busy with corporate matters, but you go ahead."

Authentic in Desire for a Better Future

A successful leader is concerned with the future of the business, and what will be required to achieve that future. A leader creates possibility. This possibility is what allows employees to engage and ultimately commit to being involved in the transformation. The authentic desire for a future that is more fulfilling and rewarding lives in the possibilities that are created together by the leader and the employees.

Part of what is so sad about failed attempts at strategic execution and transformation is the residue that remains with the employees. Usually the managers move on to another assignment or another company, but the majority of the employees remain. When a change effort fails, among the biggest causalities is the sense of possibility for the future among the employees. Repeated failures at strategic execution can "suck the possibility" out of the employees, and make them hardened and resigned that little can be accomplished. This is a tragedy for all concerned, and is quite common.

Honoring Boundaries that Matter to Others
Authenticity and self knowledge translates into the ability to see the boundaries that are in existence. These are the boundaries that need to be honored as well as those that need to be challenged and changed. Those of you who work in global or international companies have a vivid example of how boundaries differ from country to country and culture to culture. The point is to be aware that boundaries exist for groups of people that need to be honored.

There are many boundaries that need to be observed and managed. That could be an entire article in itself. However, three areas of boundary will be discussed. The first is tolerance of mistakes. The second is the chaotic nature of change and the third is what to talk about, and not talk about.

Tolerance of Mistakes
The first boundary is the tolerance of mistakes and managing how mistakes are identified and addressed. Mistakes happen in the day-to-day running of a business. Mistakes really happen in transforming a business. If the mistakes are punished, transformation will simply not happen. So the leader must develop an approach that has the mistakes identified as soon as they are seen and talked about in an open manner. It is essential that those associated with the mistake not be punished, as future mistakes will be "swept under the rug" and covert operations will commence all around. To complicate matters, a transformation will not likely

be successful until those involved with it come to appreciate the importance of mistakes, celebrate the discovery and mobilize people to learn from the situation.

The Chaotic Nature of Transformation

A second boundary to be managed is the chaotic nature of transformational change. Incremental change is usually linear and predictable. Transformational change is discontinuous, and by definition not linear. However, if managers are not careful they will respond by trying to control or reduce the chaotic nature of change in a transformation, which of course serves to thwart the transformation and push the business backwards. The manager who starts a transformation and then tries to control or thwart it when it gets too chaotic will be perceived by others as inauthentic, i.e., not a leader. A common description of this type of person is "he or she is not serious, and never was". This is a strong accusation to make about a manager, especially by key employees who work for that manager. In the end, these efforts look like "more of the same", which will make the organization even more resistant to change when the next attempt at strategic execution is made.

Knows What to Say and What Not to Say

A third crucial boundary for the leader to observe and manage is what to say and what not to say. A leader is concerned with saying what will make a contribution or a difference for those that are working to improve the business. A leader has speaking as the primary tool, so it is essential that boundaries of what not to talk about are maintained. An example of what NOT to talk about is getting involved in organizational politics. Organizational politics will not forward the leader. Further, those who are involved in organizational politics are usually not leaders and in many cases are opposed to the leaders. That is, those who engage in organizational or "palace politics" are seldom effective leaders. The converse of that seems to be accurate. Those who are unable or unwilling to be leaders are the ones who are actively involved in "palace politics". Palace politics are heightened during times of transformation as the dramatic changes that are being implemented are often threatening to those not in leadership positions. Palace politics are often directed at trying to stop the transformation and those associated with it.

Expands Learning for All

People learn around leaders. They are challenged by the questions and inspired by the attitudes, passion and velocity of the leaders. In turn, leaders learn from supporting others to learn. One of the clear signs of an authentic leader is the thirst for learning and knowledge that is seen around them. In contrast, the evidence for lack of authenticity by false leaders is what their people say, "Sure there is much that we could do better, but there is no use given (the name of person) is here". Learning comes from inspiring people to find better ways to do their jobs and improving the processes and operations in the business.

Avoids Reliance on Excuses

The greatest threat to authenticity comes from excuses, whether self-generated or given by others. That is, if a person grows up with a belief or value that a good excuse justifies an action or non-action, it is hard for them to emerge as an authentic adult. This pattern continues into adulthood and the workplace. Authentic leaders do not broker excuses or live in a world of excuses. Excuses are seen as irrelevant and a threat to successful execution. In contrast, inauthentic managers are characterized by the extensive use of excuses. I have consulted in companies where the capacity to make excuses appeared to be a primary criteria for promotion.

Let me give you an example. There was a company who prided itself as performance-based and excelling in management rigor. Each month the executives from the business units had a variance meeting with the chairman. For two days in advance, the executives focused on how best to tell their story. Then there was the all-day meeting, which was typically followed by a one-day post-mortem. The executives spent about four days a month preparing for this variance meeting. What made this more stunning to me was that there were seldom consequences of not meeting performance targets as long as there was a good excuse or story. Those business units where the executives were the most skilled presenters seemed to excel and get the additional capital for expansion, regardless of the poor performance of their units.

An attribute of non-leaders is their unwillingness to face the facts and reliance on good excuses to offset actions/no actions. I have recommended to several companies that they adopt the slogan "Result $\neq$ No Result + Good Excuse". This recommendation is based on a practice that developed where a good explanation for why something did not happen was a "pass". This was most commonly applied to expected results that did not happen, e.g., we missed the plan this month because of $\underline{X}$. What I noticed was the same business units would miss the plan each month and yet there was a new and novel explanation. These business units were not skilled at producing results, but were very clever in producing excuses.

It is common to find companies where making good excuses is considered a core skill for developing as a manager. I observed a financial services company where there were monthly variance meetings with the CEO. The intention of these meetings was to discuss performance in the last planning period on key metrics. These variance meetings were well orchestrated by various corporate staff groups, and the preparation by the line organizations were also intense. In some cases, the business unit management teams would spend a couple of days in preparation for what was about a two hour meeting. What amazed me was the time and effort spent by the staff groups in preparing their strategies to "attack" the business unit management teams. Of course the management teams spent a similar amount of effort in preparing their defenses. When I asked "what happens in these meetings", I was told that the executives who "win" are those who can tell the best stories, i.e., make the best excuses. In fact, I was told that a key factor for career progression in the company was the capacity to tell a believable story about really poor performance. Needless to say, authenticity was not a key value of executives in this company, nor was this leadership team able to achieve a transformation. It took a new CEO and "house cleaning" to accomplish that.

Accepting Responsibility Rather than Blaming Others

Authentic leaders do not play the "blame game". Rather, they step forward and factually describe what happened. To some of you this may seem obvious as the right thing to do. While it may seem obvious, it is not the management practice in many companies.

The dynamic of looking for whom to blame while avoiding being blamed is too common in business. In some organizations there is such a blame-based culture that there is a continual process of avoiding blame vs. looking for whom to blame. As one employee described it to me, "We let no good deed go unpunished." I have seen organizations where avoiding blame had been taken to the level of art form. While intriguing to watch, these behaviors in no way contribute to results being accomplished or add value. Employees notice who "dances around to avoid blame", rather than stepping up to deal directly with events in the business. I am often amazed at the frequency with which prospective leaders blatantly deny or ignore that important events happened. It is a sense that an event will go away "if I pretend it did not happen". Pretending is a clear sign of lack of authenticity and leadership. There is an old pop/rock song with the lyrics, "Yes, I'm the great pretender, pretending that you're still around …" While the song was a hit, pretenders in business are not.

I have often seen managers who spend enormous energy and time avoiding blame that it becomes a primary "organizing feature for them". So much attention is spent in avoiding blame that it is hard for employees to determine what these managers believe in or stand for. There is another song that captures this avoidance of blame. It is from the musical "Best Little Whorehouse in Texas". There is a scene in which the Governor of Texas is being confronted about the existence of a brothel in the state, which conveniently was located not too far from the state capital of Austin. When the news reporter was about to corner the Governor, he broke into a song and dance entitled "Ooh, I Love the Side-step". Too many managers are specialists in their version of the "Side-step song and dance".

Acknowledges Facts and Avoids Denial
Denial is a common trait of managers who are not effective as leaders. There is a common expression that has developed, which is a testimony of how frequently denial is used:

Denial is not a river in Egypt

Denial is a special problem if exhibited by prospective leaders. While denial is easy to do, the consequences on perceived authenticity are disastrous. Employees see the denial and quickly draw conclusions of "what this person is made of". The negative impressions created by "getting caught in denial" cannot readily be explained away or forgotten. Denial is a primitive defense mechanism, commonly used by children. We are not surprised when we see young children trying out denial. For example:

Father: Billy, have you been eating the chocolate chip cookies?

Billy: No dad.

Father: Well how did you get chocolate all over your fingers?

Billy: I do not know. I guess my sister Susie must have put it there ....

In this situation Billy's father would have chuckled to himself and then sat his son on his lap for a father-son chat about "We tell the truth in this family; do not tell me lies". At the end of the conversation the father would welcome this opportunity to teach his young son. It is a very different circumstance when the father is an executive who is dealing with managers who exhibit similar levels of denial, rather than being responsible for what is happening in the business.

Conclusion

Authenticity is at the heart of inspiring the actions of employees. Think about it, can there be any attribute that is more motivating to employees than working with an authentic leader? The employees can see that the leader is committed, which in turn serves to inspire the employees to action as well as becoming more committed.

Authenticity Self Study Guide

Summary

Authenticity is "habitual truthfulness" that shines through the leader's actions. Leaders must be perceived as being "the real deal", or authentic, if they are to be effective in strategic execution. Personal authenticity is highly correlated with effectiveness as a leader of transformation and achievement of business results.

Key Points

1. Authenticity begins with the leader being candid with self, and practicing "habitual truthfulness".

2. Self deception is the worst lie of all.

3. Authentic leaders "know themselves" (warts and all).

4. Authenticity is not an accident. Leaders strive to develop and expand their capacity to be authentic in all their dealings.

5. Leaders act responsibly.

6. Leaders practice constancy in being authentic, and in wanting to create a better future for the organization.

7. Leaders' authenticity is demonstrated in their communications.

8. Leaders go first in making personal changes that are required for success in strategic execution. They do not ask employees to make changes that they are unwilling to make.

9. Leaders honor boundaries that matter to others. The appreciation of others boundaries is a walking demonstration of consideration and authenticity.

10. People grow and learn about leaders.

11. Authentic leaders do not:
    a. Rely on excuses.
    b. Blame others.
    c. Live in denial.

Foundational Leaders

11.

Ownership

Increasing responsibility to enable employee engagement

Ownership is a heightened state of being responsible for one's self and one's surroundings. In a business, it is voluntarily holding oneself responsible for actions and business outcomes beyond one's formal authority. Employees choose to act in the best interest of the business and far beyond what they are formally expected to do.

> *Ownership is a condition of being responsible where individuals choose to be responsible in matters of the business far beyond their formal accountabilities.*

I like the term "ownership" since it conveys that individuals choose to invest what they consider precious and valuable into improving the business. I am speaking about investment of one's self in the business. The precious investment is creativeness, energy, intellect, intensity and integrity, putting friendships and personal reputation at risk and risking alienating colleagues. From the perspective of the individuals, they are putting themselves at risk with no guarantee or promise of reward. I use the term "ownership" regardless of whether the employees have financial ownership in the business or not.

For strategic execution and transformation to be successful, there needs to be a number of individuals who have committed to the success of the transformation and have taken ownership that success will be achieved. The transformation effort reaches a "tipping point" to move forward forcefully when a critical mass of employees chooses to stand for success and put themselves at stake for the future of the business. Let's look at the impact of ownership on transformation.

Distinction of Ownership

Ownership is choosing to be responsible beyond what is expected of the individual. It is a declaration that, *"I choose to own conditions, circumstances, events and situations that impact this business, whether or not I had anything to do with producing it. It happened or is happening, and I choose to own it so that I may have an opportunity to transform it."* The willingness of an individual employee to create ownership for his- or herself is a core element in a transformation. Employees choosing to be responsible in matters of the business rather than blame/denial are a building block of transformation.

Dynamics of Ownership

When one chooses to "be an owner" it literally alters that person's context, how they see the world, what they choose to be responsible for, and how they behave. Ironically this dynamic works regardless of whether the person has literal legal and financial ownership. Let's look at some examples.

Stock Ownership as Part of Executive Compensation

Have executive compensation plans that gave or sold company stock to executives made them more responsible? Has it produced the desired effect of having them appreciate the needs of other shareholders and act decisively in the best interest of shareholders, rather than in their own best interest? While there are some indications that this has happened, there are also many, many cases in which it did not happen. Rather than the executives acting in the best interests of shareholders, they instead became even more attached to their entitlements and acted in flagrant self interest. In those cases, there is little evidence that legal and financial ownership promoted "being responsible" on the part of the executives.

Ownership as Entitlement

I have owned several consulting and service companies. On many occasions I have had employees tell me that they deserved to be made an owner of the company. When I would ask them how much they were willing to pay for their ownership, invariably we got around to their answer of "nothing". They wanted to be given ownership in exchange for some other value they would create. On several occasions I went along with this, only to later regret it since the person accepted the ownership and then did not deliver the promised value. In these cases ownership was mistaken as an entitlement and prestige, rather than responsibility.

Communism

I consulted in Russia when it was still the center of the Soviet Union. At the time, private ownership of land and houses was forbidden. While this was part of the communist government's approach, there were some interesting dichotomies. This was most notable in big cities, like Moscow. The skyline of Moscow was dominated by apartment buildings, many of them high-rises of eight to twelve stories. The exteriors of many of these buildings were cement, so they were all the same off-white color. Inside, the floor plans of apartments were all pretty much the same: one or two bedrooms, a dining room/living room, a bathroom and a kitchen. Most noticeable to me was the deplorable conditions in these apartment buildings. Maintenance of their buildings was the responsibility of the government, and the people had neither the money nor access to supplies to do anything with their buildings. Further, there seemed to be little interest in improving the appearance of the buildings, as there was no "ownership".

The buildings were poorly constructed and in serious disrepair. The lobbies were usually dark, since the lights had burned out and were not replaced. It was depressing for me to go visit my colleagues and friends in their Moscow apartments. Ironically behind many of these apartments were small plots of ground where individuals could have a small garden. While these plots of land were quite small, they received much more attention and care than the apartment buildings. Again it was a sense of personal involvement or "investment of oneself".

In traveling outside of Moscow, I made an interesting discovery. Many of the people I knew were entitled to dachas. Dachas are cottages or country houses outside of Moscow. While the dachas were quite basic, the upkeep of the dachas and the surrounding grounds was remarkably better since it was the responsibility of the people who "owned" the dachas, rather than the government. There was not legal ownership, but there clearly was a condition of "being responsible". This phenomenon can be seen the world over. When people have a sense of personal involvement or investment in something, it is much better maintained.

Impact of Ownership on Leaders of Execution

Employees who adopt a state of being responsible or "being owners" have a profound impact on transformation. This ownership creates a foundation of future for the business, it alters the context to a more empowering one, it promotes choice and possibility, it enhances accomplishment, it is key to engaging other employees, and it empowers managers, supervisors and team leaders in the midst of change. Assuming this level of responsibility, or ownership, occurs only through the affect of leaders. Otherwise there is too much distrust, fear of risk, history, and skepticism for people to engage at this level.

Ownership allows people to hold themselves as responsible for the organization's situation.

Transformation happens when a sufficient number of employees create a stand of ownership and respond from being responsible rather than being at the effect of circumstances. Being responsible creates an entirely different set of possibilities for the business. This allows employees to choose to be responsible for aspects of the business that are well beyond what is expected or normal. Ownership is demonstrated through owning the past and the current situation, as well as the future of the business. Ownership allows people to hold themselves as *responsible* for the organization's situation. The state of being an "owner" (being responsible) extends beyond areas in which the employee had direct involvement; e.g., events that occurred prior to the employee coming into the organization. In fact, in some situations I have seen employees step up to own circumstances that were based on behaviors and decisions of the company decades earlier.

1. Ownership Gives Access to Responsibility for the Past
Owning the past is assuming ownership of the history of the business - that is, to choose to be responsible for whatever has happened in the past. This ownership

applies both to things that were positive and negative. This is essential since many employees are attached to something that happened in the past. In the case of "glory from the past", the employees want to return to the good old days. Unfortunately, we can never go back, especially in a business. The glory days are gone, and while they are celebrated as part of history, there is actually very little about the past that will support a transformation since a transformation is created from and for a future that is quite different than the past/present.

Employees may be attached to or stopped by negative things that happened in the past; e.g., actions by managers that were perceived as acting in bad faith. A common example of this is when managers are meeting with union leaders to support participation in a transformation effort. Rather than the discussions being on the

Ownership
1. Gives access to completing the past
2. Creates foundation of future
3. Alters the context
4. Promotes choice
5. Enhances accomplishment
6. Engages employees
7. Empowers managers, supervisors and team leaders

current business circumstances and the needs of the business, the discussions focus on previous times in which the union members felt betrayed when they attempted to cooperate with managers of the company. While these situations are unfortunate, they also need to be left in the past. What is called for is ownership of the past by employees and managers (i.e., being responsible for the past allows the events of the past to be acknowledged and completed). This is a crucial event in starting a transformation.

While ownership of the past is challenging, being responsible for and owning the present is even more difficult. This includes being responsible for the current performance of the business. The tendency is to blame events and people in the past for current performance. While these accounts may make a good story, it does little to prepare the business for different performance in the future and transformation.

Ownership of the present is a key building block for transformation. An "owner" will take possession of the circumstances and create something even in the toughest times. Mounting a strong response to the circumstances and situations that a team encounters is evidence that ownership is present. Flying by the seat of your pants is not a demonstration of ownership. Ownership leads to jolting colleagues, teams and in some cases entire organizations into responding to opportunities and threats. People with

> *Ownership of the present is a key building block for transformation. An "owner" will take possession of the circumstances and create something even in the toughest times.*

ownership can be counted on to watch out for the well-being of other employees and the business. This is not to say that they treat other employees as if they are babies still in the cradle. Rather, they honor the commitment, skill and talent that their colleagues bring to the situation.

Part of owning is seeing that other employees are being developed, which may involve putting them in challenging situations. Being stretched in order to grow is much preferred to pampering or coddling, and is ultimately a part of the passage into creating ownership.

2. Ownership Creates Foundation of Future
Vision of the future authentically expresses what employees are looking to see. Making that future visible is the role of formal and informal leaders.

A business that succeeds in transformation does so because of the intense commitment of many to achieving that future. If there is not clarity about or credibility of the proposed future, little success will occur. Ownership creates energy in people. That is, the verve of employees at different levels of the organization is what brings the future into existence for employees.

> *The future is seen as achievable by employees because of the owners of their colleagues and leaders. This authenticity of commitment is demonstrated by ownership of both the future and the actions required to achieve that future.*

Future is the essence of communication and engagement. If a person or group of people can see themselves in a future, then they have a choice to become personally involved. *Future* is what engages employees. Self-engagement by employees is a matter of choice. People are most likely to choose to self-engage into a transformation that will lead to a compelling future. The view of the compelling future occurs through the actions and speaking of others.

That is, the person has chosen to sign up for the vision and to become involved in the actions that will be required to make that vision a reality. The desired level of engagement is reached when the employees say, "I own this future, I will be engaged to see that it is fulfilled, and I can be counted on because I own our/my future here. "

> *When formal and informal leaders own the future, their personal commitment is evident.*

When formal and informal leaders own the future, their personal commitment is evident. When they do not own the future, their personal commitment is notably absent and is replaced with much talk and a "likely story". If the leaders do not own the future, then there is little chance that they will effectively enroll the employees. The employees can usually tell when their leaders own the future or not. For example, a manager that appears to be glancing over the shoulder looking for approval from others will not inspire movement toward a future. This manager is likely to be a hindrance through jumbled communications. Rather than articulating a future that allows others to see a possibility for themselves, this manager will give confused messages such that what is being said about the future is actually rendered useless.

3. Ownership Alters the Context

Context is the beliefs and invisible premises of an organization that are shared through behavior and conversations of employees. Context determines what the employees can hear and see inside and outside of the company. Since context shapes how things occur for the employees, you can see how it will make tremendous impact on what employees see as appropriate actions and speech. Further, it shapes what alternatives that the employees can see.

Altering the context is of prime concern to those who are producing a transformation in a business. The past/current context has produced the current behavior, performance, processes and strategies. To attempt to produce a transformation without changing the context is futile. The question then is how to best alter the context. The answer is that context is altered through conversations by people in the business. Among the best ways to produce the right conversations by employees in the business is to have them create ownership. That is, being responsible for the past, present and future of the business.

> *A successful transformation happens because of choice.*

Ownership alters context by giving employees an entirely different view of what has happened as well as a strong commitment to impact the future. Ownership is a key enabler of changing the context.

4. Ownership Promotes Choice

A successful transformation happens because of choice. Choice is essential in creating possibility and opportunity. People *choose* to become involved and to do heroic things to assure success. This occurs best when groups of people in the business have created ownership, which in turn allows them to create choice. It is hard to overstate the importance of choice. When employees and teams choose, rather than being forced into having only one option, a much better outcome is likely.

Ownership evokes continued challenging. Choices are designed to provide possibility and opportunity, rather than deal with scarcity. A parallel for this is to compare the difference in a tree growing in the woods and what can be done with it later. When a forester or lumberjack looks at a tree, they can choose to cut down or harvest the tree. That is a choice. When the tree is cut down it becomes timber. When the tree is taken to a saw mill, it is cut into various size pieces. At this point, what was once timber has now become lumber. The person running the saw has more choices as to how the tree will be cut up. Using a computer program that gives an estimate of the optimal means of cutting up the tree, the employee running the sawing station is able to choose the best alternative. After sawing, the various pieces are gathered by like size and prepared for shipping. When the lumber is delivered to the building site, once again many, many more choices are available. What was once a tree becomes many different parts of a house, from the structural support of walls and rooms to beautiful decorative parts, e.g., the gable at the top of the house.

Strategic executions and transformations are much less likely to succeed if a command and control approach is used. Command and control is designed to achieve compliance and predictability. By its very nature, a transformation is unpredictable and unexpected.

5. Ownership Enhances Accomplishment

You will not see outstanding levels of accomplishment without ownership. Ownership leads to effective set-up of businesses as well as projects and work teams. One aspect of ownership is that it leads to making clear the accountability in the organization for accomplishing specific results.

Elevating the results of a team and the organization is a sign that ownership is present. It may not always be clear what the leaders did or said to inspire the performance, but nonetheless the results are visible. I have

> *Elevating the results of a team and the organization is a sign that ownership is present.*

seen numerous times when leaders enter a team or organization and there is immediate impact. It is thought the impact of leadership bulges out through the actions and results of the team. The only identifiable explanation for this bulge or expanding of performance is the leader. In contrast, teams and organizations which undertake actions to dramatically improve their performance and do not have strong leadership seem to end in tumult. There is significant confusion and disorder among the employees, and very little business results.

In business units and project teams that are off-track, an excellent place to look is at the ownership of the team leaders. Often what you will discover is that the team leaders do not own the project and/or the results. This occurs for a variety of reasons. In some cases the person was never committed to the project results and did not make that known. Often the person says "yes" and begins immediately looking for a personal escape route so as not to get blamed when the results are not achieved. Other managers begin with good intentions and then lose their way. Often this comes from encountering something that they cannot figure out how to resolve and/or discovering that the support for this project is not as strong as was initially thought. This is often the case when the team leader discovers that the executives who created the project will quietly step away so as to not have to deal with and be responsible for any controversy that is created by the project.

A business leader is often called upon to make rapid response to an unexpected development. The leader will call upon the team and organization to act competently and decisively to the challenge. Less mature managers or those who have not created ownership are afraid to challenge a team or organization to respond rapidly, lest permanent damage might be done. A more experienced manager appreciates the elasticity of people's commitments. With strong commitment of employees, an organization is able to resume its normal shape spontaneously after being stretched or squeezed, while meeting a challenge. Based on the confidence in the leaders, the employees demonstrate a willingness to take control of the situation and generate solutions and strategies that will be executed.

The questions that often face a team in the darkest hour are: "Can we take possession of this situation and create something that is extraordinary?" and "How do we convert this situation into an opportunity for learning and triumph, rather than slithering away amid a slew of excuses?" Taking possession of the moment is a key aspect of ownership. When things are not going well, ownership is most needed, and the call for leaders to step up and raise the morale and performance of others is most crucial. There is a sense of being determined and exhibiting what has been called deterministic behavior. That is behavior that will address the circumstances and situations over which the team has control or ability to influence. The team may not be able to influence global economic factors and market trends, but there are areas where the team can influence. Getting to work on those areas that we can impact is also a sign of ownership.

6. Engages Employees

Employee groups and teams that have ownership are empowered to be in action and are resourceful. Empowered and resourceful people find a way to accomplish results. Empowered and resourceful teams are usually the reflection of team members with strong ownership. Please do not hear my use of the term leader to imply that the person is an executive or senior manager. Some of the most important leaders are front-line employees. These leaders' ownership gives them a unique view. In turn they are able to use this view to assist others in seeing a broad view of the situation as well as innovative approaches to delivering the result.

Employees who are engaged and unwavering in their commitment are desired in many companies. Unfortunately, the reality of employee commitment and engagement is lower than expected. It seems that many employees have become numb to the demands for change and performance improvement. Rather than being strong tall oaks, many are like willows that bend whichever direction the wind is blowing. Rather than being based on their commitments, they go with the winds of fashion and pretend to be involved and committed. This pretense is in lieu of a commitment, and it shows. These employees appear to be willing to be involved, and agree that "some of the ox need to be gored" (changes need to be made). These employees are interested until they realize that "their ox may be one of those gored". At that point a very different set of behaviors emerge. This sudden shift invariably occurs in the midst of implementation, which is one of the reasons that strategic execution is so challenging.

Flagging levels of interest and commitment are a classic sign of a group of employees who do not believe that the managers and supervisors have sufficient investment or ownership of the actions that are required to achieve a transformation. When employees see that their direct bosses are mumbling about the change program, they are likely to assume that the bosses have less investment than is expected. It is likely that the bosses will attempt to rig the implementation so that it looks like they tried to comply, but for some unexpected reason the implementation failed. Employees often assume that the supervisors and managers will blame the failure in implementation on uncooperative employees. This seems to be the standard way it works in many companies.

7. Empowered Managers, Supervisors and Team Leaders

Ownership of the transformation is important for managers, supervisors and team leaders. Ironically, mid-managers and supervisors are often caught in the most awkward situation during strategic execution and transformation. They are expected to maintain controls and levels of performance in the business while transformational levels of change are occurring in the business. Often these people become frustrated and threatened by the changes that are occurring. I say this is in large part because they have not created a condition of ownership. In their defense, I should point out that these mid-managers and supervisors are often overlooked as the transformation is being launched. I think that it is essential for these managers and supervisors be supported and trained so they can be active in their ownership. If that does not happen, it is painfully obvious to employees in their organization.

The managers, supervisors and team leaders who do not have ownership will invariably behave and speak in such a way that gives clear communication that they have not "bought in" nor have ownership. Savvy employees will see this manager as being "off target" and not to be trusted. It is not that the manager means harm; it is just that the initiative and teams under the direction of this manager will flounder. Managers who have created a condition of ownership for themselves are aware of the consequences and risks they are asking employees to take in order to achieve the transformation. Managers with ownership have credibility with others because they have thought through the dynamics and consequences that may occur for employees and teams.

A sign of the ownership of the managers is the environment they maintain around them. A true leader focuses on keeping a healthy environment in the business, both figuratively and literally. A leader keeps the waters pristine, while a pseudo-leader lets the water become brackish if not polluted. A leader attends to the health and quality of the dunes on the shore, while the pseudo-leader focuses on self and ignores the health of the beaches and sensitive areas for employees. Employees that are not looked after will not create long-term value for shareholders.

> *A sign of the ownership of the managers is the environment they maintain around them. A true leader focuses on keeping a healthy environment in the business, both figuratively and literally.*

Conclusion

Ownership is a state of being responsible, or a condition of being responsible where individuals choose to be responsible in matters of the business far beyond their formal accountabilities. That is, employees choose to act in the best interest of the business and far beyond what they are formally expected to do. For strategic execution to be successful there needs to be a number of individuals who have committed to the success of the transformation and have taken "ownership" that success is achieved. The transformation effort reaches a "tipping point" to move forward forcefully when a critical mass of employees chooses to stand for success and put themselves at stake for the future of the business.

Ownership Self Study Guide

Summary

1. Ownership is a state or condition of being responsible, or a condition of being responsible where individuals choose to be responsible in matters of the business far beyond their formal accountabilities.
2. Employees choose to act in the best interest of the business and far beyond what they are formally expected to do.
3. For strategic execution to be successful there needs to be a number of individuals who have committed to the success of the transformation and have taken "ownership" that success is achieved.
4. The transformation effort reaches a "tipping point" to move forward forcefully when a critical mass of employees choose to stand for success and put themselves at stake for the future of the business.

Impact of Ownership or New Level of Employees Being Responsible

1. Alters the context, which in turn changes what a person sees and how he or she perceives it. This in turn impacts how a person will behave.
2. Provides a basis for organizational transformation which is required for success in strategic execution.
3. Gives access to completing matters from the past of the organization and people's experience of how they were previously treated.
4. Provides a foundation for a future that is different from the past.
5. Promotes choice, which is a key ingredient in successful implementation.
6. Enhances a person's or team's accomplishment.

7. Engages employees at a new level of participation and causes indigenous leaders to emerge.
8. Empowers managers and supervisors to be more effective as leaders.

Questions to Consider
1. Can you think of times when you had a change in your perception of being responsible for something? (Could be on sports team, community organization, etc.)
2. What has been important to you in developing a heightened sense of being responsible or ownership?
3. Can you think of a time when you were around a change effort in which there was not clear ownership, or sense of who was being responsible? What happened? What impressions did you have?
4. Can you think of an attractive future without having some commitment to that future?
   a. Probably not. Otherwise it sounds like a campaign promise from a politician or someone's "good idea", but not real to you.
   b. Chances are you experience that a future does not seem real until you have taken on some level of responsibility for it happening, and then it becomes much more real.
5. Can you think of times when other leaders gave you a choice? What was your reaction and experience? Usually we are much more likely to choose to commit to something when we have a choice.
6. Can you think of times when you were told that you needed to be committed to something? How did that work for you? (Usually we are not prone to become committed simply because we are told to do so).

Foundational Leaders

12.

Continual Development as a Foundational Leader

Developing as a Foundational Leader is a life long journey. As long as you are alert and active, you will be learning leadership. The agenda and settings will change, yet leadership learning continues until your mental facilities begin to fail you. You are never a "finished product". You are never completely "turned out". Ironically in business as you get better as a leader the challenge become larger and more complex.

Leadership ONLY occurs in some form of action. Among the most important actions is communications. Others will act because of some communication they are having with a leader. Developing yourself as a leader involves finding ways to observe yourself in action. Leadership occurs in action. Learning leadership comes from leading. Leading is NOT the same as learning about leadership. While there is an incredible amount written about leadership, little that is written actually contributes to developing yourself as a leader. Learning <u>about</u> leadership comes from reading articles, books, and going to classes. Ironically what I am about to say is that you will learn little leadership in reading articles or books. You may learn new concepts or ideas, but real learning comes only from "being in the game on the field, leading and working with leaders".

Where Learning Leadership Begins

For most leaders, learning to lead begins early with childhood involvement in things that mattered, taking action and inspiring actions of others. While there is no single path in development of Foundational Leaders, it does seem that early life experiences are important. What do you remember about your own childhood that has shaped you as a leader?

- When did you have your first business experience? For example, mine was mowing the grass in neighbor's yards, having a paper delivery route and painting houses.
- When was your first "management job"? For example, mine was grade 10 in high school when I became an assistant to the route manager for the Dallas Time Herald (the afternoon daily newspaper in Dallas at the time).
- When did you have your first failure as a prospective leader? For example, mine was also in grade 10 when I ran for an office that I thought I would win, and lost badly.

Each of us has a unique path in development as a leader and someone who is committed to excellence in our endeavors. Take a minute and think about your own journey.

Some of you followed a formal path, like scouting, sports, and school activities. For others of you it is more personal, like being a care giver for an elderly grandparent, involvement in mission trips to other countries, volunteering to work with less fortunate children, tutoring in elementary schools, etc. For still others it was the earliest jobs where one was able to watch effective leaders as well as ineffective supervisors. For most of you there is some of all of the above.

The development of Foundational Leaders is a continual process and is very personal. Learning to lead ultimately involves observing your actions to see which actions has the desired impact on others. There are no easy solutions or recipes. It is a blend of intense desire to learn to lead, exposure to life experiences and willingness to learn from situations that do not work out as planned.

Thinking About Your Own Development as a Leader

Take a moment and think about whom have you experienced as inspiring you? What did they do, and what was the impact on your life? As a way of capturing this for yourself, think of at least three instances in which you were inspired by another. I encourage you to write this down in the chart provided on the next page as we will use your personal data as we work through this discussion. To give you an example, I am listing two of the people who were influential in my development in the following chart.

Example

	Who inspired you?	What did they do?	What impact did this inspiration have on you?	What action/results did you accomplish as a result of this action?
1	C.W.	Reassured me that I was capable, up to the task	Gave me confidence to move forward aggressively with my project	Created an outcome far beyond what anyone thought was possible
2	Steve	Redirected and gave mild confrontation	Got me back on the right path and kept me from wasting much time and effort	Able to complete this project in shorter time than anticipated and produce excellent results

Chart One – Your Experience of Being Inspired

	Who inspired you?	What did they do?	What impact did this inspiration have on you?	What action/results did you accomplish as a result of this action?
1				
2				
3				

What do you see when you look at your answers? Do you see that another's speaking and actions had a positive impact on you? Do you see actions and accomplishments that would not have occurred without the actions of another AND you responding to the inspiration? If you then think back on the persons whom inspired you, what do you think was their commitment at the point that the inspiration occurred? Can you see that their commitments were demonstrated in the act that you experienced as inspiring?

From this look back into your history, you can see that for another to inspire you is a contribution to you. What I would like to explore now is when you have inspired others. Using a similar chart, think of at least three times that you inspired another person. If you cannot think of three instances, then there is one of two situations to consider:

1. Stop being so humble – This is an "adult conversation" that you need to be aware of and master. Inspiring others is your job as a Foundational Leader and you need to be aware of what you are doing and the impact it is having on others. Observing how you inspire others and then the actions that others take as a result of your inspiration is a crucial data source for you as a leader. It is critical that you can watch this for yourself as well as the other leaders in your organization. If you can observe this phenomenon at work in the actions and speech of others, you can become an excellent mentor to other leaders in your organization.

2. If you have never inspired three people you should seriously consider not going forward with trying to be a Foundational Leader at this time. I'd suggest you go out and get into relationship with people in your area of work and look for ways that you can inspire them and support them in being great. Once you have gained that experience and knowledge, then you may benefit from this conversation.

Chart Two – Your Experience of Inspired Others

	Who did you inspire?	What did you do?	What impact did this inspiration appear to have on the other person?	What action/results did the other person accomplish as a result of this action?
1				
2				
3				

I hope that you are getting an appreciation of inspiration as it occurs in your work, as well as how much impact you are able to make when you inspire others. Now let's look at some of the different approaches to inspiration.

Approaches to Inspiring Action in Others

We have established that a Foundational Leader develops in action, and that the leader's actions inspire others to take actions that produce extraordinary results. Now we want to look at a range of options that leaders have for inspiring others. Consider the following approaches to inspiration:

1. Asking great questions – Great questions provide a door to action. Great questions open up your thinking and challenge you to think in a different way. It expands horizons and views. Leaders leave others hungry for better ways to accomplish a result or better ways to speak about something that is possible.

Leaders open people up to consider new ways and to look for ways to reach beyond the current circumstances.

Please note my use of the adjective great in front of the work questions. Too often what I heard asked as questions is not great, does not inspire the other person and often is not even a real question. Too often I heard "statements" worded as if it is a question yet all those around clearly understand that it is an instruction or direction rather than a valid question.

2. Challenging – leaders often issue challenges to others. The challenge is to do more and to find ways to improve the performance. Foundational Leaders are not all "sweetness and light". Rather they often challenge basic assumptions and beliefs as a way of opening up conversations and thinking.

3. Guiding to get you on the right track and avoid unnecessary pitfalls – leaders actions are often to correct direction and trajectory. The methods vary greatly, and yet the consistent theme is "fine-tuning direction".

4. Confronting, dislodging and interrupting – transformation is not a smooth linear process. It requires dislodging the status quo and interrupting familiar ways of working. In the early days this is often dramatic or stark. Yet it is essential. Leaders appreciate that this is part of the job and more with speed and force to create the interruption. In contrast, non-leaders are often squeamish about possibly upsetting others and are unwilling to take the needed actions. This inaction is a disservice to the change effort and the employees.

5. Accompanying you during the most difficult times – this is walking along side of you not doing it for you.

6. Assuring comments - Affirming confidence in you and your team.

7. Assisting you with technical solutions that you could not otherwise have seen. This could include making additional resources available.

If you remember the examples I gave for those who have inspired me, I say they used the following approaches to inspiration:

Example

	Who inspired you	What did they do?	What impact did this inspiration have on you?	What approaches to inspiration did this person use?
1	C.W.	Reassured me that I was capable, up to the task	Gave me confidence to move forward aggressively with my project	Assuring, expanding my horizons
2	Steve	Redirected and gave mild confrontation	Got me back on the right path and kept me from wasting much time and effort	Confronting / interrupting, and guiding

Please look back at your answers to the first chart (Chart One – Your experience of being inspired) and label the approach to inspiration that you saw this person do. Enter your data on the first two columns in the chart below. What would you put in the third column?

Chart Three Identifying Types of Inspiration

	What did they do?	**What impact did this inspiration have on you?**	**What type of inspiration was this?**
1			
2			
3			

As you look at your experience, I imagine that you find that there are a number of different approaches that others have used to inspire you. I also imagine that there are certain approaches that you like better than others. For example, I doubt that you listed "belittling and public humiliation" as the approach that others have used to inspire you that you remember fondly. Let's now look at what others need to be inspired.

Conclusion

Developing as a Foundational Leader is a life long journey. You are never a "finished product". You are never completely "turned out". Ironically, as you get better as a leader, the challenge becomes larger and more complex. Learning leadership comes from leading. Learning <u>about</u> leadership comes from reading articles, books, and going to classes. You will learn little *leadership* in reading articles or books. You may learn new concepts or ideas, but real learning comes only from "being in the game on the field, leading and working with leaders". The best setting for developing your leadership is to be involved in a project with clear boundaries and clear statements of extraordinary levels of results to be achieved, and to develop yourself based on what is required to inspire others to act in ways that will achieve the expected results. That is the best classroom for leading available on the planet.

13.

Foundational Leadership Competencies

Given that most Foundational Leaders find the need to recruit and develop other Foundational Leaders to enable execution, let me present a partial list of the leadership competencies that I see present in leaders who are successful in strategic execution. Please remember that I am focused on those who already have the proper foundational commitments and appear ready to step forward to provide Foundational Leadership. Also, please remember that many of the best Foundational Leaders are NOT in management positions.

While there are many lists of competencies around, most that I have seen are general and not focused on what it takes to lead strategic execution. These competencies are not complete in sequence or order of importance, as some occur simultaneously. All are important.

Foundational Leader Competencies
1. Foundational commitments
2. Clarity of values
3. Ability and discipline to think strategically
4. External perspective
5. Distinguishes facts from opinions
6. Distinguishes context
7. Bases strategy and execution on results
8. Creates multiple paths for strategy
9. Is alert to consequences of prior actions
10. Inspires others
11. Develops others
12. Is responsible for current conditions
13. Distinguishes action from activity
14. Results, results and then more results
15. Assures discipline, integrity and rigor are present
16. Looks for cross boundary opportunities and acts when possible
17. Builds in sustainability

1. Foundational Commitments

Does this person appear to have foundational commitments? This topic is discussed in great detail in three chapters earlier in this book. Please look at those chapters for more information if this is not clear.

2. Clarity of Values

Foundational Leaders are sourced by their values. These values give rise to their thinking, speaking and actions. Leaders "walk the talk" of their values and are concerned that others see them acting consistently with these values.

Do you see this person being the manifestation of the vision of the business and the values for achieving that vision?

3. **Ability and Discipline to Think Strategically**

    Does this person demonstrate strategic thinking? Strategic thinking begins with learning how to think critically or to think for self independent of the current convention and popular view. Once critical thinking is in place, it is the ability to see paths that could be followed to accomplish a result. That is, developing pathways and a plan in one's thinking. I often see very bright people who are incapable of figuring out what to do, since they cannot see action in their mind much less string together a series of actions into a pathway. Those who lead successful strategic execution can see a pathway for implementation long before a plan is formally developed.

4. **External Perspective**

    Leaders in strategic execution must be able to think from others' perspectives. This includes thinking from the perspective of customers, communities in which the business occurs, employees, shareholders and other stakeholders. Thinking from this external perspective includes appreciating what these different constituents expect, need for their own success and want. Inward focus and thinking makes strategic execution much more difficult than needs be, and is in many cases a fatal error. Does this person demonstrate capability to think from external or "outside-in perspective"?

5. **Distinguishes <u>Facts from Opinions</u>**

    Successful strategic execution is fact based. Too often there is confusion in facts and opinions. What's more, employees often state opinions as though they are facts, and actually think they are describing a fact. A great question to ask is, "Do you think or do you know?" *Think* implies that it is an opinion, while *know* means that it is a fact. Does this person keep facts and opinions as distinct, or are they frequently confused?

6. **Distinguishes Context**

Successful leaders are able to see the existing context and the impact the context is having on behavior and results. In addition, leaders must be able to articulate a new context that will impact how employees hear the invitation to become engaged and participate in achieving exceptional results for the business. That is, due to the changed context employees will act, talk and think in different ways. These different ways of acting, talking and thinking lead to extraordinary levels of business results. Does this person appear to appreciate what context is and how it works? Have you seen them bring clarity to conversations by pointing to differences in context, as well as identifying the context that is needed for future success?

7. **Bases Strategy and Execution on Results**

Does this person distinguish the specific results required for success? Foundational Leaders in strategic execution identify specific measureable results that are to be achieved by the execution. These results become the focus point for all those involved in the execution. Are this person's actions shaped by results, or is it simply a matter of talk?

8. **Creates Multiple Paths for Strategy**

Developing successful strategy includes being able to see multiple paths for implementation. Often I have heard successful leaders say, "You can't have only one pathway for implementation, because if you do, you are at grave risk of something unexpected blocking the path." Another way of saying it is "always have safe routes home", which will allow success in implementation even if the unexpected occurs.

Leading strategic execution requires being able to see multiple paths for implementation. There is danger if the leaders lock in on one right path in their thinking. This type of linear thinking leads to rigidity, failure to see threats on the horizon, and limited opportunities to expand the scope of the execution and achieve even greater level of results. Among the options to be considered, a leader always wants to have "a safe way home". That is, a means to assuring success even when circumstances do not turn out as favorably as expected. Does this person create multiple options and path for getting things done, or are they prone to have only one way?

9. Is Alert to Consequences of Prior Actions

Can this person see the consequences of prior actions? Do they seem to be thinking ahead "a couple of moves on the board"? Foundational Leaders need to be able to see the consequences of actions that are taken, and not taken. This includes the intended consequences as well as the unintended consequences. Success in execution usually depends on the ability and willingness to deal with unintended consequences.

10. Inspires Others

Is this person inspiring others to act in ways they would not otherwise act to produce results they would not otherwise produce? When I use the term inspire I do not infer to an emotional outpouring or reaction. The term "inspired employees" does not mean that individuals are floating around the workplace with sweetness and light. This is not a tent revival where people are standing and clapping. I use the term *inspire* to mean taking actions that they otherwise would not have taken to produce business results that otherwise would not have happened.

When I speak about a leader inspiring others in the organization, I mean that a leader breathes life into the organization that would not otherwise have been there. People in the organization have unique feelings, paths for action and thoughts as a result of interacting with a leader. What makes it unique is that it would not have happened if the leader had not been present. The act of inspiring is to bring something into existence that gives openings for action to others in the organization. Hence, when you look for evidence of leadership it is wise to look at the people around the leader rather than at the specific actions of the leader.

11. Develops Others

Does this person have a track-record of developing others? Showing others how to act as leaders is essential. Of course, developing others will invariably develop the leader as well. It is like the old adage that the one who teaches learns more that any of the students. If you cannot find a list of people this person developed, let me suggest you go to work right there. Look around to see whom this prospective leader can contribute to. Whom can that person challenge to be more than they are currently being? Who can the prospective leader "water and then watch them grow"? The people are likely all around the prospective leader, whether they appreciate it or not. If the prospective leader does not see anyone to develop, let me suggest have this person go stand in front of a mirror and sort out what they need to do to have these people show up around you. It is not likely that a prospective leader will inspire others without the capacity and experience of developing others.

12. Is Responsible for Current Conditions

Foundational Leaders are willing to be responsible for current conditions in the business, whether or not they had much to do with how the business got into this condition. Is this person willing to do that, or do they always have an excuse or story. If a person looks at their circumstances as a reflection of leadership and does not allow blame or excuses to enter into the deliberations, they will find very useful information for execution. Access will be given to perspectives and options that otherwise would not be accessible. If a leader is willing to think from a position of "things around me are this way for a reason and I have had much to do with those reasons", this leader will gain valuable insights on current context as well as future context.

13. Distinguishes Action from Activity

Action leads to results. Action is a result unfolding. Activity does not necessarily mean that a result is going to be produced. Often activities lead to more activities, rather than results. People being busy does not mean that a result is in midst of happening. A leader of strategic execution needs to be able to distinguish action from activities. Can this person tell the difference? Does it show up in actions?

14. Results, Results and then More Results

Does this person have an uncanny way of achieving better results than expected? Is there a track record of results, results and more results? Or is there a track record of less than expected results combined with an excuse or good story?

15. Assures **Discipline, Integrity and Rigor** are Present

While inspiration is essential for success in execution, so is discipline, integrity and rigor. Do you frequently see those attributes around this person? Can you count of this person being discipline to actions, insisting on the highest level of integrity and working with rigor? If yes, you likely have the makings of a Foundational Leader. If not, it is unlikely that this person will make the grade.

16. Looks for Cross Boundary Opportunities and Acts when Possible

Is this person provincial in their actions? Do they tend to think that their area or group is the best and others are inferior? Does this person seem to network across organizational and geographical boundaries? Foundational Leaders will ultimately be required to skillfully build constituencies and work across organizational boundaries as the execution moves forward. Does this person seem suited to this approach?

17. Builds in Sustainability

Does this person look for ways to enhance implementation and assure sustainability? Sustainability is not an accident or an afterthought. It is designed in from the beginning. The results achieved in the strategic execution are more likely to be sustained if the employees in the organization were at the heart of the accomplishment. The people will see opportunities to build on the accomplishments, and will be much more tenacious in protecting the gains made.

Conclusion

Foundational Leaders are called on to recruit and develop other Foundational Leaders to enable execution. This list of seventeen competencies is based on what I see present in leaders who are successful in strategic execution. Please remember that I am focused on those who already have the proper foundational commitments and appear ready to step forward to provide Foundational Leadership. Also, please remember that many of the best Foundational Leaders are NOT in management positions. This list should provide the basis for good developmental conversations as well as assisting with selection.

14.

Engaging Others

A key to success of Foundational Leaders is quickly engaging other Foundational Leaders. Isolation is deadly. There must be other leaders around. They key is to assure that the right people are being enrolled as Foundational Leaders. A major criterion for selecting the "right people" is that the person has chosen to lead. They have made this as a free choice and are acting accordingly. People who act as if they had no choice in the matter will only slow down if not derail the execution efforts. Those who are expected to lead must be committed to leading, and eager to face the challenges that will come. The freedom to choose is essential for a person committing to leading. The person of whom leadership is wanted must always have a choice to participate or not. Effective leadership comes ONLY with freedom of choice and ultimately commitment. Persons who feel forced into a leadership role will predictably fall short of expectations, if not fail.

The seven steps in engaging others to become leaders:
1. Communicate the future for the business
2. Communicate how the strategy will be executed and consequences expected
3. Distinguish leadership in strategic execution
4. Assure that management position and leadership are not seen as synonymous
5. Communicate the challenges that can be expected
6. Allow the person to choose
7. Once choice given, explore ways to develop and support the person

Choice is Essential

Each person who is to become involved in leadership should have the freedom to choose whether or not to take on this role. This may seem counterintuitive, as often people are in positions that are expected to be involved. Nonetheless it is a mistake to assume that someone is committed to becoming a leader simply because of the position they currently hold. In many cases persons in higher ranking positions are often the most resistant to changes that will occur as part of the strategic execution. Often I find myself in conversations about this dynamic and hear an executive or manager say "But they should be committed". While the point may be valid, simply because someone should be committed does not in any way mean that they are or ever will be committed.

"Commitment is what transforms a promise into reality...It is the daily triumph of integrity over skepticism."

Abraham Lincoln

Commitment is an act of volition or choice. Commitment is not something that one can be forced into. People will momentarily act based on direction or threat, but that does not mean that they are committed to continuing the actions once the direction and threat are removed. So it is with leadership. Leadership is a choice that must be made by each person. Further, like any commitment it is a choice that one gives oneself on a day-to-day basis. Leadership is not a position or title. It is a condition in which one commits to influencing and inspiring others to act in ways that will produce extraordinary business results.

The question then is how one chooses to become a leader. What are the questions one asks oneself? I will present the factors to be considered in making this decision, and hope that you will seriously consider that each person must have a choice in the matter because:

> Choice is a crucial element in transformation. All those who are involved should do so because they want to be involved. No one should be coerced or forced into involvement.

> If a person feels like they do not have a choice in the matter, they will say yes to participation and yet not be able to fully commit. Often they adopt a context of "I was forced", "I didn't have a choice", "They made me do it", etc. All of those contexts are weak and result in weak leadership.

> If a person is not participating as a consequence of choice, they will not be successful. They will find it very difficult to create and exhibit the level of commitment required for effective participation. Personal involvement will become increasingly challenging and difficult to the point that it evolves into dread, frustration and sabotage of the transformation.

> Leadership is needed from the management positions.
> a. If you are in a management position and cannot in good conscience commit to the transformation and choose to be involved, your duty is

to make this public and find some other role to play where you are not being asked to participate in leading a strategic execution and transformation.

b. If you say you are willing to be a leader and then do not follow through, you are creating a problem of integrity that will hamper the efforts of other leaders.

Steps in Assisting Others Choose to Become a Leader

1. **Communicate the future to which commitment is being sought. Allow each person to discuss this future to see if it is one to which they can choose to commit.**

2. **Communicate how the strategy will be executed and the expected consequences of successful execution.**

3. **Distinguish leadership in strategic execution.**

4. **Assure the person does not hear leadership and a management title as synonymous.**

5. **Communicate the challenges that can be expected in being a leader in this effort. Assure the person appreciates what is being asked and the consequences of taking on this role.**

6. **Allow the person to choose, and to make this choice from personal commitment. Avoid any sense of obligation or threats.**

7. **Once a person has chosen to be involved, explore ways to develop and support that person.**

1. Communicate the Future to which Commitment Is Sought

It is essential to articulate the future so that it can be heard and seen as accessible. This conversation wants to be interactive and not rushed. Be cautious not to push, but rather allow the person to ask questions. Also watch for assumptions that may come into the conversation. Assumptions are the enemy of clarity and commitment.

2. Communicate Strategy Will Be Executed as well as Expected Consequences

Articulate the business case that calls for the strategic execution along with the specific actions that are anticipated. In some cases you will have these conversations in the early days when the strategic execution is still in development. That is fine. Describe what you can and also how you would like to see this person involved. Also, talk about the outcomes that are expected from successful execution along with the strategic positioning and organizational improvements that are desired.

3. Distinguish Leadership in Strategic Execution

Begin by describing what makes a leader. One option is to work with the meaning and origin of the word *leader*. This allows you to move through implied assumptions that if not identified will impact the conversation. As an example of identifying the meaning and origin of the word *leadership*, let's look at the <u>Oxford Dictionary</u> definition.[10]

> *lead¹ /li;d/*
>
> *. v. (past and past part. led /lEd/)*
>
> *1 cause (a person) to go with one by drawing them along.*

---

[10] Oxford Dictionary

2 show (someone) the way to a destination by preceding or accompanying them (usu. lead to) be a route or means of access to a particular place.
3 culminate or result in. (lead someone to/to do something) be someone's reason or motive for.
4 have or experience (a particular way of life).

The first word in the first definition gives us a terrific insight into leadership. A leader is *"cause."* Let's look at the definition of cause. It is "Cause - n. a person or thing that gives rise to an action, phenomenon, or condition. Reasonable grounds for a belief or action."

When we look at the definition of *cause*, we first see that it is "a person or thing that gives rise to an action, phenomenon or condition."

A leader gives "rise to actions." If we look further, we see that this "rise" is not only action but also a phenomenon. Phenomenon is defined as a fact or situation that is observed to exist or happen, especially whose cause was not easily anticipated.

Transformation of an organization is certainly a phenomenon. This transformation of a company does not occur naturally. It happens only because of the intervention of leaders.

I particularly like that the word *condition* is used. What is transformed is the *condition* of the organization. The *condition* is changed so as to allow dramatic improvements in business results.

When we look at the end of the first definition of lead (leader), what is fascinating about that portion of the definition is that the focus is on causing a person (or organization) to go along with them *by preceding or accompanying them.* This suggests that a leader must precede those in the organization in making changes. In other words, if a transformation is to occur, the leader must participate in that transformation. There is no hiding out for a leader in a transformation. Not only must the leader be involved in the change, but she or he must also do so in a public manner. How else can the leader "show the way to a destination by preceding or accompanying" the people in the organization?

The second definition of leader also gives us an insight into a leader's role in transforming a business organization. The definition reads: *to lead someone to/to do something*. Leadership is about getting people in the organization to *do something*. In fact, it is getting the people in the organization to do something new that will produce a significant result. In leading a transformation, the people must act to produce a significant result and change the essence of their work and the organization. Not only is this challenging, but look at how the leader goes about getting the people in the organization to act: the definition continues...*be someone's reason or motive for*. The leader has to *be* someone's reason or motive for. People in the organization will act, based on the leader's *being their reason and motive for acting*. For a person who has grown up in company that has a command-and-control culture, it is unnatural to think about *being* a group of people's reason and motive for acting. It is much easier to give a command or make an order. What is required for managers who have grown up in a command-and-control company environment (and most have) to make this change is a transformation of themselves, personally. That leads us to the third definition.

The third definition is *to lead people to have or experience (a particular way of life)*. Organization culture is having a particular way of life at work. Changing organizational culture is creating a different, particular way of life at work, and clearly this happens only when a leader is involved.

4. Leadership is More Than a Title

In many companies the term leadership is included in the position title. There has been an interesting increase in the use of the word *leader* in job descriptions and names of management teams in companies in the western world. This is *our regional leadership team*. This is our *lead geologist*. She is our *group leader*. Even so, that means nothing when it comes to being a Foundational Leader.

While the use of the title *leader* has increased, I see little evidence that the number of leaders or the effectiveness of leadership has actually increased. That is because being called a leader and being a leader are worlds apart. It is only those folks who are *being* leaders, as contrasted to those folks who have titles of leader, whose companies achieve the transformations they must have in order to be successful.

5. Appreciating the Challenges in Transformation

Strategic execution and transformation of a business means literally changing the very essence of the organization. This change is necessary to allow the business to succeed and thrive. It is by definition a large scale change. In addition to being large, it is also difficult. Many organizations need to transform but only a few actually accomplish the transformation. Most fail to achieve the promise of the possibility of transforming their organization. That is, only a small part of the possibility that was present for improving performance of the business and impacting the organization is accomplished. Rather than accomplishing an extraordinary result in business performance and becoming a transformed organization, most settle for a compromised level of business improvement and a watered-downed version of the envisioned organizational change.

Strategic execution is very challenging to the leaders because transformations are *caused* by the leaders and accomplished because of the actions of people throughout the organization. The challenges of *leading a transformation* should NOT be taken lightly. Too often I see managers who say all the right things but appear to be unwilling to do what is needed to achieve the transformation. This includes being willing to:

- Ask people of a lesser rank to step up and take the actions to accomplish the transformation.

- Challenge yourself to change.

- Challenge yourself to grow as a leader and a person.

- Challenge yourself about your issues with control, engagement of others, risk and trust.

- Challenge what you think you know about the business. Be open to other points of view and to the possibility of discovering that the business is not exactly as you have previously considered it to be.

- Challenge prior decisions that have been made, especially those you were involved in making.

- Question processes that you like and may have helped create.

- Relinquish your "right answers" for how the transformation can be best be achieved.

- Let go of the informal privileges of your position in the organization, e.g., being deferred to when you give an idea and wanting to have the last word on any subject. Are you willing to "check you title at the door"?

6. Allow the Person to Discover if They Can Choose to Be a Leader of Strategic Execution

Allowing a person to choose includes asking them to be honest and thorough in their deliberations. I encourage each person to answer the following questions:

- Can you choose to be a leader of transformation?

- Are you willing to let go of the comfort and familiarity with how you do the job today and embark on a journey filled with chaos, risk taking and uncertainty?

- Is leading a strategic execution right for you?

- Are you willing to do what it takes to be a leader?

- You might say, "How can I make such a decision without knowing what all is involved?" Well, that is the essence of what it means to choose. You make a commitment even though you do not have a complete list of all that is involved nor a money back guarantee that it will all work out as you would like.

- Are you willing to publicly commit to the future success of the organization even though you do not now know how it will be achieved? Perhaps the most challenging aspect of leading a transformation is that you are called upon to commit to the organization's achieving results even though at the time you make the declaration you do not know how you will accomplish the result. It is this act of speaking based on your commitments that will open up the possibilities for extraordinary results in approaches and involvement of additional people in the organization.

- Are you willing to speak based on your commitments that others will step up? It is through their involvement that actions and unprecedented results will occur. Ultimately this will allow you to precede and/or accompany those around you in making the changes that result in a powerful transformation of the business.

- Are you willing to stick with it when the going gets rough? It is a disservice to your organization to say that you are committed to a transformation and then to back down from your commitment when the going gets rough. I can promise you that the going will get rough. The only question is your willingness to be creative in approaches to the difficult situations and your willingness to persist in creating leadership even when the going gets tough. It has often been said that many can lead when things are going well, but the true test of the leader is what happens when the going gets tough. Performance in tough times is what distinguishes a real leader from a pretender.

- What do you choose?

Those are the essential questions that each person must answer for themselves as part of choosing to become involved. I encourage you not to rush these deliberations. Do not rush it. It is better that a person takes time to think about the role and the implications. Also be cautious of the people who quickly say yes. Often this person is trying to be agreeable and loyal without actually thinking about the challenge ahead. The "quick adopters" often become problematic in the midst of execution, which of course is precisely the wrong time.

7. Development and Support that Would Be Useful to Increase this Person's Effectiveness.

When I look starkly at the many companies that I have interacted with who are attempting a transformation, I see that they have badly underestimated the challenges of leadership. I find myself asking the following questions:

- How come it is so difficult for managers to see the challenges and opportunities of the business and decide that a transformation is required?

- How come so many managers back off and settle for watered down changes rather than driving for transformation?

- How come there are so few leaders?

- Why don't people who are bright, charming managers step up to the opportunity of becoming a leader?

- What makes certain people turn tail and run from the challenge of leadership?

As I ask myself these questions I come to the following observations:

1. **Most managers have not been trained to lead.**
   They have been trained to control and manage, but not to lead. Leading is a very different phenomenon, and calls on quite different experiences and skills than managing.

2. **Leadership is often scary business.**
   For most managers it looks like putting at risk all of the perks and rewards that come with their hard-earned position.

3. **The leader gets to go first in changing the particular way of life.**
   Again for many managers this is moving away from a rigid command-and-control culture and creating a different or new *particular way of life at work.* This change begins with the leader, and the changes are made in public.

4. **The courage it takes to publicly lead a transformation is immense.**

The lack of such courage is, in part, why so many change efforts fail. Let me give an example. I was working with a company that had a classic command-and-control culture. The executives all had impressive credentials. Most were graduates of excellent universities and business schools. The CEO was a graduate of one of the US military academies and a well-regarded law school. His military training made him a perfect fit for a command-and-control culture. His physical appearance was impressive. He was tall with grey hair and carried the bearing of authority. He looked perfect for the role of a CEO, as if he had been selected by Hollywood casting.

However, when the company was facing the need for him to lead a transformation, he was lost. All of his instincts were of little use, and his experience led him to take actions that were inconsistent with what he was saying. There was one incident that captures the essence of the challenge. The company had frequent meetings in New York and, therefore, had leased a very nice apartment in Manhattan. The apartment could be used by any of the executives, although, of course, the CEO got first choice when he was in the city. The apartment management provided cleaning services but not always on a daily basis. Consequently, there would be times when an executive would come into the apartment and find dirty dishes left in the sink. The CEO found this irksome, and he wrote a memo to all the executives and managers. In this memo he announced that, from that day forward, if any executive were ever caught leaving dirty dishes in the sink, that executive would be denied future use of the New York apartment. What made this especially telling was that the dirty-dishes memo was circulated at the same time the CEO was issuing a memo to all executives and managers announcing that the company culture was in need of change and was changing immediately to a more participative culture. The changing-culture memo exhorted the managers to take risks in leading the change. As the executive who showed me the two memos side-by-side I observed, "The message of the two memos are in conflict, and the signal that the command-and-control culture was not changing is very clear." Needless to say that CEO was not successful as a leader of change.

5. **Leading a transformation requires developing other leaders**
Being a leader includes being a mentor and sponsor of others. It requires standing on the sidelines like a coach watching others play the game. It involves resisting the temptation to want to run on the field and jump into the game.

6. **One leader can't do it alone**
One leader cannot transform an organization alone. The leader will need much help, and, in fact, will need many others to step up and lead. A transformation requires a cadre of leaders. These are people throughout the organization who step up and provide leadership at the moment it is required. It is interesting to me that often the leadership comes from unlikely persons in unexpected roles. A phrase that captures this is: Look for leadership where you do not expect it and do not be surprised when you do not get the leadership from those of whom you have the highest expectations.

7. **Promoting leadership by the front-line**
I have observed that the most inspirational leadership often comes from non-management employees. These front-line employees are closely involved with the customers, makers of the products or providers of the services. The passion they bring to their work is amazing, and the challenge in leading a transformation is to unleash it. You may be thinking, "Well, that may have been the case in other companies, but you haven't seen the dolts that work here."

I suppose there is always a first time, but I've yet to see a company that did not have front-line employees who step up and provide outstanding leadership. I have seen uneducated hourly workers who live in small rural towns that appear to be "not too bright" or "lazy." Yet these employees turn out to be the most amazing employees when they are encouraged to lead. When I am told about employees who are dolts, I have a very good read on the type of management that has been provided as well as the absence of leadership.

8. Dealing with colleagues and friends.

It would be advantageous if the leader could look at her/his direct reports and know that this group was in full support of the change effort and actively involved in becoming effective leaders on their own. While that would be advantageous, it virtually never happens. Rather, the most difficult group of employees to engage in the transformation is usually the direct reports of the leader. There is usually considerable resistance to the direction that the leader is attempting to take the organization and personally to the leader.

In a cartoon called Pogo, there is the classic saying: *We have met the enemy and the enemy is us.* In seems that in the world of organizational transformation we could modify that saying to be: *You will meet the enemy and the enemies are your direct reports.* It is a major mistake for a leader to assume that the direct reports are on board, regardless of what these direct reports say.

It is much easier and politically correct to blame the failed change effort on the employees rather than a lack of courage in managers.

Conclusion

Choice is essential to successful leadership in strategic execution. There is no question that achieving a transformation is challenging. At the same time it may also be the most exhilarating experience in a person's career. Many leaders that I have worked with look back on the challenging times in leading a transformation as among the highlights of their work life.

15.

Developing Others as Foundational Leaders

Leaders guide others in skillful actions that accomplish results and are the origin and source of strategic execution and transformation. Success in execution occurs when there are leaders throughout the business. It does not happen because of one celebrated CEO or skilled site manager. It happens because a network or team of leaders work together to make things happen that otherwise would not have happened. Developing leaders throughout the organization becomes a crucial step in transformation.

Developing leaders throughout the business

One player does not a team make. Leaders are needed throughout.

Let's look at an example. The Los Angeles Galaxy of Major League Soccer signed a true superstar in David Beckham. The team paid an incredible amount of money for Mr. Beckham. When he and his celebrity wife Victoria (Posh Spice) came to Los Angeles it was true media frenzy. Those games in which the LA Galaxy were playing with Beckham on the team became "hot ticket" items. While David Beckham's presence on the team made major impact on ticket sales, it did not affect the team's winning record. The team was floundering near the bottom of the table (league standings) when he joined, and remained there throughout the season. Again in the second year the team did not make the playoffs, and rumors began that Beckham may be looking to return to a European team.

One excellent player cannot overcome mediocrity of the team. I'm sure you can think of many other similar examples where there was much excitement and hype when one player joined a team, yet that one player could not carry the entire team. The quarterback who does not have protection from the offensive line will not win games. The baseball pitcher who is excellent cannot win the games if his team does not score runs. The teams that win do so because of the contribution of the team – of a group of people who come together to produce excellent performance. So it is with strategic execution.

A business succeeds with strategic execution because of the contributions of groups of people. These groups of people will not make the contribution absent leaders. Leaders must be developed on the job so they can inspire their colleagues to take extraordinary actions. Ultimately strategic execution is successful because of a cadre of leaders throughout the business. Therefore, success in strategic execution is dependent on development of leaders throughout the business. Often those who emerge as the most potent leaders are not in management or supervisory positions. In fact, they may have been viewed as "opponents" of management in the past. While they may not have a history of being friendly with all managers, they do have credibility and respect of their fellow employees. They have informal leadership credibility and can be developed to be excellent leaders of strategic execution and transformation.

Leaders are the source of success in strategic execution and transformation. Leaders create clarity of purpose, appreciation of shared values, and an articulation of the future that it engages, and enable those in the organization to take actions that will lead to results. Leaders create clarity of purpose based on the results that are needed and promised for the organization. Leaders get their own being from their foundational commitments as well as the commitments that they have made in regard to the business.

The shared values that are articulated and come to be appreciated by the people in the business come from the leaders commitments as well. The values say what we believe in as an organization, what is important to us, and how we can be counted on. Values for leaders will always have a couple of elements. One is doing what we say we will do. The second is results, or as one leader told me "Results, Results, Results". It is not that leaders are not compassionate people who care about their employee's safety and well being. Most do care quite deeply. In addition they appreciate that employee's safety and well being is intimately related to achieving excellent business results.

Organizations achieve results that were otherwise not going to occur because of their leaders. If the desired level of results could be accomplished through doing nothing out of the ordinary and maintaining the status quo, there is no need for leadership. Leadership is required when the results that are wanted and needed will not occur absent some intervention. The intervention that produces the results is the role of leaders, and the evidence that leadership was present. If the results are not being accomplished, then the leaders are not getting the job done. While that statement may seem harsh or judgmental, I invite you to think along with me as to what that statement makes available and possible to a person who is committed to being a leader.

Leaders create other leaders

This simple statement goes to the heart of leadership in strategic execution and transformation. Leaders of transformation will create other Foundational Leaders. That is, on a moment-to-moment basis those involved in strategic execution are called on to be Foundational Leaders and to develop other leaders. Being a leader requires acting, listening and speaking in ways that inspire others to step up and become leaders. When groups of people are inspired and taking actions that will produce unprecedented and unexpected levels of results, that is the evidence that leadership is present. When other leaders are emerging, that is evidence that leadership is present.

Attributes of Prospective Leaders

The easiest way to develop additional Foundational Leaders is to identify people who are already credible with their peers and effectively providing leadership, even if in an informal manner. It is much easier to build on accomplishments and strengths than to start from scratch. I am going to share with you the attributes that I look for in advising on whom to select for development as Foundational Leaders.

Attributes of Prospective Leaders:
1. Personally involved
2. Overtly committed to the future of the business
3. Unconstrained by events in the past
4. Congruence in actions and speech
5. Personal growth
6. Ability and willingness to communicate
7. Engaging others
8. Bias for action
9. Skilled in dealing with difficult employees

1. Personally Involved

Does this person get personally involved in interactions with others? Do others seek out this person to have them involved with their team or task? Is there a notable pick-up in energy when this person enters a discussion?

People are inspired by direct access to leaders. It is through conversations and interactions with their leaders that each person in the business comes to choose to be involved in the strategic execution/transformation. Employees make this choice based on confidence and trust of the leaders and what the leaders stand for. This cannot be accomplished in isolation or from afar. It ultimately happens because of personal interactions and/or assuring comments from other employees whom this person trusts. People choose to follow leaders based on what might be called "belly to belly" interactions. That is, being close in proximity and having a sense of shared commitments. That will not happen if there are not leaders in the proximity. Watching a talking head on a web cast or video will not inspire people. It may provide an introduction and give information, but alone it will do little to inspire people. That happens through personal interactions with leaders. That is what makes it essential that Foundational Leaders are developed throughout the business.

2. Overtly Committed to the Future of the Business

Has this person overtly demonstrated their commitment to the future of the business? Does the commitment of this person appear obvious to others? Is this person willing to put what is best for the business and the operation ahead of personal agendas and concerns?

Foundational Leaders work from a future that is based on their personal commitment. They are committed that the strategic execution will be successful. This success will produce a much improved future for the business, employees and in many cases, their communities.

Standing for the future means that the person makes public commitments to others about the future and what impact achieving that future will have on others. This taking a stand is a demonstration of the person's willingness to be a Foundational Leader. Commitment to achieving this future is the basis for communication and enrollment of others, and without that they do not have the necessary tools to do the job. If a person is unwilling to make explicit their commitment to executing the strategies and achieving the future, they will not be successful as a Foundational Leader.

3. Unconstrained by events in the past

Does this person seem "clean" when talking about problems that the business has had in the past? Does this person openly talk about events from the past as being in the past, rather than something that is to be handled in the future?

Foundational Leaders

Often the incidents from the past that need to be completed involve lack of coherence between what leaders say and what they do. Let's look at some examples of this:

- The site manager proclaims commitment to safety, and yet walks through the plant without wearing the proper safety gear. (Ear and eye protection as well as hard hat if required).

- The executive flies into a location for meeting with local management on a very expensive private jet, and then "flogs" the local managers for not exercising tight cost controls.

- On a visit to a facility, the executives insist on staying in another town because none of the hotels in this town are nice enough. The implied message is that this town is OK for you to live and work in, but not for me to spend the night in.

- The strategy calls for dramatic growth and yet all the metrics are about cost control. At the end of the year those groups that managed their costs but did not grow are rewarded more than those groups that did achieve growth but had higher costs.

- The strategy calls for dramatic changes, and yet there are no changes in how this person works. If the prospective leader is a manager, there is little change in how the areas reporting to this manager are working.

Foundational Leaders can count on having to deal with events and perceptions from the past for which they were neither involved nor responsible. The task is to get whatever happened in the past resolved for those involved.

4. Congruence in Actions and Speech

Does this person's behavior mirror what they say? Is there credibility in the organization for this person? Is the person considered a "straight shooter" who does what he/she says?

Foundational Leaders "walk the talk". That is, the leaders behave consistently with what they are asking others to do. They lead by example. They do not ask employees to do anything that they are not willing to do. There is coherence between what the leaders are saying and how they are behaving.

5. Personal Growth

Is this person mature? Has the person had life challenges and faced adversity? Does the person seem stronger as a result of the challenges they have faced? Does the person appear eager to learn how to be more effective?

Transformation requires personal change. A transformation requires dramatic change by the people in the organization to learn to work in a different way, to alter processes, and most of all to raise the level of performance. Most employees will experience some discomfort with giving up old ways of working and having to learn new ways. Foundational Leaders are not immune from this change, and in fact need to be out front in making the personal changes. Employees are aware of many of the changes that their leaders will need to make if the transformation is to be successful, and often keep a close eye on the leader to see what happens. The leader's actions speak much more powerfully than their words.

> *"If we are to change, first we must change."*
> **- Gandhi**

Developing as Foundational Leaders will require personal changes, and leaders often experience these changes as uncomfortable. I must admit that I am still amazed at how frequently leaders are unwilling to face their own discomfort with changes, and dig their heels in rather than make the needed changes. Needless to say, change efforts led by those who are unwilling to make personal changes are severely hampered if not doomed.

6. Ability and Willingness to Communicate

Is this person articulate in their own way? Is this person willing to communicate even when it is uncomfortable? Does the person's communication lead to action?

A Foundational Leader's primary job is communication. This communication should be focused on translating the message to the employees and helping them see why the transformation is a good thing, as well as what is wanted and needed from them. Often what the leader is communicating is initially hard to hear since it is so different from the past and present realities. At times it is shocking for the employees to hear. Nonetheless, this communication is crucial.

7. Engaging Others

Do others join in when asked to do so by this person? Does this person have a viable constituency group within the organization? Do others listen to what this person has to say?

Strategic execution and transformation is successful only when a critical mass of employees decides that it is in their best interest that the strategic execution succeeds, and joins in. Employees are "engaged" or enrolled when they see that the transformation is meaningful for themselves and the business. Each employee who becomes involved in the transformation will engage with a series of questions, e.g., what is the company trying to do, why now, what does this mean to me personally, will I have a job when this is over, etc.? Employees engage with a transformation on a very personal level. If the leader speaks about the transformation as a concept, and does not make the translation for the employees, it will make it more difficult for the employees to determine if the transformation is a good thing and if they should become involved. The leader must "build the bridge" from the concept of the transformation to the specific requests for actions and involvement.

The transformation is made meaningful by the leader engaging and inspiring groups of people, who in turn engage and inspire others. To be successful in a transformation, employees need to be more engaged and committed than they were prior to beginning the transformation. This engagement will not occur if they do not consider the transformation to be personally meaningful, and essential to the future success of the business.

8. Bias for Action

Is this person prone to act? Can this person be counted on to see what is needed, and then communicate/engage others to accomplish the task? Is this person willing to get involved in resolving contentious situations? Is this person viewed as being firm but fair?

Employees will watch Foundational Leaders to see what actions are taken when events occur that are clearly a challenge to the strategic execution. Employees will look to see if their "so called leaders" become like ostriches and put their heads in the sand when something embarrassing and unpleasant occurs. Acting like ostriches is a primitive form of behavior that psychologists call denial. It is pretending that something did not happen. If I don't see it, I do not have to deal with it. As one employee put it, "I used to think that denial was a river in Egypt till I saw these guys". (This is a pun on "the Nile" being a river in Egypt).

9. Skilled in Dealing with Difficult Employees

Foundational Leaders will be called on to deal with difficult employees. Whenever possible the leaders want to engage these employees to determine if they can be brought on board. Often the most effective leaders were once annoying, challenging employees. Let's look at some of these challenges:

- Complainers or "whiners": One type of interaction is with people who frequently complain. The first step is to listen to the complaint. In some cases the complaint is an accurate description of a circumstance that is in need of attention. Those are the easy ones.

- Poorly formed requests: A second category of complaints are actually a poorly formed request. The person is asking for something, and often wants to contribute to the transformation but is speaking in a manner that makes it difficult to hear. Effective listening by the leaders will usually allow this complaint to be re-expressed as a request for inclusion, and from that point it is also easy to accept and get the person included.

- Endless or pointless complaints that will not get resolved: The tough ones are when a person or group has a recurring complaint. When the leaders listen to the complaint they cannot hear a viable circumstance in need of attention. Rather what is present is undifferentiated complaints, also known as whining. This situation eventually calls for the leaders to address those who are complaining and ask them to be responsible for their speaking and to find a way to contribute. Easier said than done in some cases.

- Holding on to problems from the past: One of the behaviors of managers that cannot be tolerated is blaming past failures and mistakes on the employees, and implying that the same thing will happen again. The issues from the past need to be talked about and resolved. If the conversations persist after several attempts to resolve the past, the Foundational Leaders may conclude that they are dealing with something that is intended to sabotage the future. The person who is committing the sabotage may or may not be aware of the consequences that they are creating. It may not be intentional. However, that really does not matter as the damage from the sabotage will be the same regardless of the intent.

- Confusion about accountability for results: The managers who are accountable for the business are accountable for accomplishing success in strategic execution. It should remain clear who is accountable for the quality of the results. With that clarity, the managers want to be very public that they are asking others to join in with them as they work from a commitment to be responsible in seeing that strategic execution is successful. They want to make public that management cannot achieve anything without the active support of employees, and together they can be much more successful than working apart or against each other.

- Confusion of how the strategic execution/transformation ties into the business: Some will try to keep strategic execution/transformation isolated from or separate from how business is done. Common expressions are "this is the flavor of the month", "program de jour", "keep your head down as this too will pass". The inference is that this is a temporary phenomenon that will have little lasting impact on business operations. Ironically, that very statement is often given as reassurance to managers and discouragement to employees. It is what some managers hope for and employees dread. Foundational Leaders should then make sure that the transformation is connected to business results in the minds of the employees. A transformation that is not connected to specific business results will soon turn into a corporate program and lose effectiveness. Then the Foundational Leaders need to engage with those who keep insisting that this is a temporary program to see if they can "win them over". While it is not necessarily recommended as an approach, I did find humorous the statement that a site manager made to one of his direct reports. He said, "Please understand that what we are implementing is not temporary, and if you keep insisting that it is, what may become temporary is your employment here."

Selecting the First Cadre of Leaders to Develop

The challenge you will likely face is not having enough qualified candidates if you use the attributes that I have just described. If you have more than enough people who fit those attributes, you are a lucky person. Chances are your selection is more complicated because you do not have all the candidates that you need. This calls on you to use your intuition along with whatever data is available. To explore your intuition, ask yourself if you can see this person being a remarkable leader within the company in a 12 month period. As an example, some of the most remarkable leaders I have seen were union officers who were included in strategy and turnaround plans. These men and women grasped the financial challenges as well as the market challenges as fast as any manager on the project. They were well respected and connected in the organization, and able to rally employees to take needed actions much quicker that anyone expected.

One other thought. The resources and time you invest in developing people should be one of your best investments. If your intuition is that a person will be well worth the investment, go for it!

Foundational Leaders

Formal Development Programs

Here is the paradox. Many companies do not have the amount, type and level of leadership that is needed for the business to successfully execute its strategies and deliver the needed results. The leadership talent that is ready to step into key positions is not in the company. Going outside the business to hire leaders can be used only so often, and with mixed results. What then is a business to do? The obvious answer is to "grow our own leaders ASAP".

While this solution may be obvious, actually implementing it is a big challenge. In this chapter, I will point toward the reasons these leadership development efforts often do not deliver the expected benefits and then provide suggestions for improvement.

Learning Leadership

The challenge facing each person in development is to determine what it will take to be a leader, determining if being a leader is something worth pursuing and then investigating the options for developing and learning leadership.

Notice that the expression used is "learning leadership", not learning *about* leadership. As you will see this is a key distinction for developing as a leader. Learning leadership involves developing the capacity in oneself to inspire others. It is developing an appreciation for what others need in order to understand the desired course of action and to commit to acting and behaving in desired ways. Learning to lead also involves confronting one's characteristics and tendencies that would stand in the way of leading.

Foundational Leaders

Learning about leadership is a very different path. Much has been written <u>about</u> leadership. There are some excellent authors, like Warren Benis, John Kotter and Noel Tichey, who have made excellent contribution to the thinking about leadership. There are also some absolutely dreadful books on the subject, e.g., Richard Nixon's book entitled Leaders. The business section of book stores are full of books <u>about</u> leadership. A Google search on leadership will produce literally thousands of references.

The predicament for most business people is that learning <u>about</u> leadership will make little difference in their ability to lead others to produce exceptional business results.

Caution on Developing Leaders Based on External Characteristics

Many leadership books describe personal characteristics of the person and what the person should have. These characteristics begin with what I call the "external characteristics". Let's look at some examples.

1. Physical appearance of the person. I have seen executives who look like they stepped right out of Hollywood casting for the role of CEO. Men who are tall, athletic, distinguished looking are assumed to be leaders. Women who are serious looking and carry themselves with pride are thought to be leaders. While it is nice that a person is attractive, it has little to do with their effectiveness as a leader. Some of the most attractive managers I have seen have been among the weakest leaders. Conversely, some of the best leaders I've seen were nothing special to look at.

2. Dress for success – For quite some time "Dress for Success" was viewed as critical. While tailors and those who sell business attire still promote

this concept, most of us do not realize that the quality of a person's clothing is not a reflection of that person's leadership capabilities.

3. Education – Another example of external characteristics is that the person should have an MBA degree from a prestigious institution. In some cases that is taken to extreme assuming the person's leadership capability is determined by the prestige of the university the degree is from. While MBA level training is valuable, it does not equip one to be a leader. Most MBA curriculums have little formal class work on leadership.

4. "Leadership for Dummies by Dummies" – Much of leadership development is taught by people who are not business leaders and have little appreciation for what actually occurs "on the field of play" when a leader is working. Often these instructors are human resource department employees who are interested in leadership as a concept, yet are unfamiliar with leadership in action. Further, what is required to be a leader is not only foreign, but threatening to these people. That is why they are in human resources rather than the front-line.

5. Theory based – Leadership theories are interesting and useful as long as viewed as a theory. Too often the latest leadership theory becomes so popular that it is talked about as if it is true, or valid. That is when the disservice begins.

6. Other examples of appearance – External characteristics are that the person should excel in golf or tennis, and preferably both. In addition, they should live in the "right" neighborhood, be members of the "right" clubs and drive the "right" kind of car. In fact, they should have the "right" kind of wrist watch. These are but a few of the "external characteristics" which

are applied in certain companies. While these "beliefs" persist, there is no data that suggests that any of these characteristics make any difference in identifying leaders.

Limitations of Relying Only on Internal Characteristics

In addition to the external characteristics, there are also beliefs about internal characteristics that will identify leaders. Internal characteristics are personal attributes that are valued in a business and thought to demonstrate leadership. These internal characteristics include:

1. Having good communication skills is a classic – This description is usually given to someone who is articulate and forceful in their speech. Often this person uses language and their voice to position themselves well. This is the person who makes a presentation in a meeting that is clever and entertaining. However, skills in making presentations and speeches does not a leader make. The key question is not how well does the person talk, but rather how well does the person listen. Ironically, how well a prospective leader listens is key to how well others in the organization will listen to their attempts at leadership. Effective communicators are great listeners. Effective communicators use this ability to listen to others to develop an appreciation of what is going on with their listeners and to interact directly with their listener's concerns. Most leaders are effective in communications, and yet simply having communications skills alone does not make a leader.

2. Knowing the answer to every question – "Knows all the answers" is often viewed as a proxy for intelligence and depth of knowledge of the business. While these two assumptions may well be correct, it does not indicate that

a person is or will be an effective leader. Rather, knowing all the answers seems to work against people who are attempting to be a leader. One of the secrets to effective leadership is the recognition that one does not have all the answers, and that even more essential is the action to be taken based on having gotten the right answer. Effective leaders often say "I do not know what the best answer is", and ask a group of employees to determine the right answer along with the best approach to implementation.

3. Strong analytic skills – Possessing great analytical skills is important as a staff person and as a manager. However, having great analytical skills alone does not necessarily make an effective leader. I have often seen people with strong analytical skills struggle to be a leader since they quickly get to their view on the right answer, and grow impatient when others in the organization take longer to reach a conclusion. For a leader knowing the right answer is often the "booby prize", since the results are achieved by others implementing the right answer to gain results.

4. Loyalty – My favorite mistaken internal characteristic is *loyalty*. Loyalty is admirable and desirable. No question. Yet for all its desirable attributes, loyalty does not produce leadership. Loyalty produces loyalty and leadership produces leadership. My comments should NOT be taken as undervaluing loyalty. I value it. Yet I want to make sure you know that loyalty is different than leadership.

Let's look at the definition of loyal and loyalty:

loyal

☐**adj.** showing firm and constant support or allegiance to a person or institution.

loyalty

□**n. (pl. loyalties)** the state of being loyal. □ a strong feeling of support or allegiance.

It is excellent when a person *shows firm and constant support or allegiance to an institution*, and the values and commitments of an institution. This kind of person will be an excellent employee, and may well be an excellent leader. Please remember that my view is that leaders are wanted and needed at all levels of the organization, especially the front-line employees. Front-line employees who are asked to participate and provide leadership are a tremendous asset to a business. In fact, as we will discuss later, they are the secret to transforming a company to achieve high performance and then sustaining that performance.

The discussion on loyalty becomes more complicated when we look back at the definition and see that it says *showing firm and constant support or allegiance **to a person** or institution*. It is in the case of the <u>loyalty to a person</u> where the mischief may come in. If the person to whom the loyalty is given is a leader with the proper commitments and values, then that is great. In most cases employees personalize their loyalty to individuals as much as institutions. The "company's management" is usually seen as the next two levels of supervision and management. Beyond that our managers becomes a concept. So, if the next two levels of supervision and management about an employee are committed to the right outcomes and demonstrate the right values, everything will work out fine. Unfortunately, that is often not the case, especially when a business is attempting to transform its performance. Too often there are individuals in the chain of supervision and management that are committed to developing their own powerbase at the expense of others and performance of the business. They are committed to their own success regardless of the impact on others, doing it their way, and do not have the right values. Ironically, these are the same people who so demand loyalty from their people. They insist on loyalty from others, and view it as the most important attribute. Hence my warning to be cautious when loyalty is described as evidence of a person's attributes as a leader.

While there is no question that loyalty is a desired value in a person, it is NOT any indication of a person's ability to lead others. When I hear loyalty used as a description of a person's leadership capability, I immediately become suspicious that this business has a very political environment that puts more emphasis on command and control than it does achieving outstanding performance. Loyalty often translates into "You will not challenge me, embarrass me by asking tough questions or make me uncomfortable by suggesting something that I did not think of first". Such a definition of loyalty is the antithesis of leadership.

Is the Answer to Read What Leaders Say About Their Own Successes?

I have noticed that some of the best leaders I know do not read much if anything on leadership. In fact, I have developed a practice of developing summaries of books or pieces of work that I want my clients to learn rather than assuming that they will actually read the book. It is not that my clients are lazy, rather that they are so busy and have so much to read on a wide variety of topics that they simply do not have the energy to read in depth on any one subject, including leadership. Ironically I have also noticed that those managers who read a lot on leadership are not necessarily the best leaders. I have become suspicious when I hear that a person is very interested in this leadership "stuff" and has read a lot on the subject. My observation is that the track record of people like this in being a leader is not very good. They are often quite versed in the theories of leadership and can talk about leadership. They however are not very good at being a leader.

Let me share an analogy: I am a sailor, who loves to race sailboats. My bookshelf is full of articles and books on racing sailboats. I have DVD's, computer simulations and paintings of sailboats all over my office. However, none of these makes much difference when I am in the boat with my hand on the tiller just before beginning a race. At that point in time trying to remember what I read last will make little difference, and in fact usually sets me up to make a blunder. The problem with sailboat racing is that a blunder before the start of a race is very hard to overcome, at least in very competitive fleets. Sounds a lot like running a business doesn't it? I was working with an excellent executive in an oil and gas exploration company. He told me that the quality of performance for a year in a business unit was determined by March. That is, the results for the year was determined by the plans and actions were in midst of implementation by the end of March. Over time I came to see that the advice I had received was correct. It also reminds me of starting a race. It is essential to have leadership present from before the beginning of the race all the way to completion.

There is a lot written about what leaders do. For example, leaders communicate, they walk around and meet with people, leaders "empower" others, leaders demonstrate respect for others and etc. The implication is that if you do enough of these things, you will be a leader. The challenge is that while many leaders do most of these things, simply doing these things will not necessarily make you a leader. Too often I have seen managers decide that they will communicate, only to discover that they do not get the response that they were expecting. There are a variety of reasons for this undesirable response, including not speaking like they were actually talking to the intended audience.

Speaking to the front-line employees like you are talking to a group of managers is a sure way to fail. Often we hear employees say, it was the typical "managers talking to themselves with no concern or interest to me". It is not that front-line employees are disinterested in the condition of the business or proposed directions. Far from it. Often they have more at stake in the success of the business than the managers. It is that the managers do not actually talk about the business and what is needed. Rather they describe concepts and strategies that are not actually linked to what is needed and wanted from employees.

Walking around meeting with employees will in and of itself not actually do much for the employees or the business. I have repeatedly seen executives and managers who walk around and talk with employees, only to have the employees see them as less and less of a leader. Often what is found is that after talking to the supposed leader, the employees are more discouraged about the future of the business than they were before the encounter.

Similar discussions could be had about empowering employees. Often I hear managers talk negatively about "empowering employees". "I don't know what that means". "They've got a job that pays well, what more do they need from me to do a good job". "Are we supposed to let the inmates run the asylum?" These are all common expressions from managers who belittle or ridicule the concept of empowering others while at the same time insisting that they already have empowered their employees. Empowering employees may actually mean giving them the power to take actions that the manager personally does not understand and would probably do another way.

"My employees like me" is often confused with demonstrating respect to the managers. Most managers have little appreciation for how they are viewed by their employees. Some assume that acceptable comments and scores on company sponsored 360 degree feedbacks is a sign of admiration and respect. I frequently see that not to be the case. Rather it is simply that "smart" employees know how to respond on company sponsored assessments when there is no evidence of a commitment to change behavior on the part of the involved executives and managers.

One theme runs through all of these comments about what a person does in hopes of being a leader. It is that employees see not only what the leader is doing, but the context in which the actions are occurring. That is, while they pay attention to the actions and behaviors of supposed leaders, they also observe the conditions, circumstances, environment and values that are present. I call this the context. Employees observe the context for the behaviors. This context is created by how the person is being. The one-line phrase that captures this is "I cannot see what you do because of who you are being".

Mimicking the Stars May Not Be the Answer Either

In business we have become enamored with "star leaders". There are many high profile executives who are described as if they are rock stars, and receive "rock star" levels of compensation as well. Ironically, most of these "star leaders" do not actually deliver the expected results. In his book *Good to Great*, Jim Collins debunks the myth of excellent value creation coming from the star CEOs. The best cases of value creation did not come from the high profile companies with star CEOs, but rather from more mundane companies with unassuming CEOs. The most successful companies were led by CEOs that most of us have never heard of. I am not saying that we cannot learn from listening to and reading works by high profile CEOs. In some cases we can. However, in many cases what is written by these famous executives is of little use to other executives.

> *Let me give you an example. Many years ago I was working in Detroit with one of the big three automotive companies. At the time Lee Iacocca was a celebrity for the turnaround at Chrysler. On the road driving into town from the airport there was a large billboard advertising Iacocca's best selling book. The billboard featured a larger than life picture of Iacocca standing with his arms crossed and looking out. It was as though he was standing there looking down on those who drove in front of him. Iacocca's book made very entertaining and inspiring reading. The problem is that it described what he did in the past in a unique situation and gave little perspective on what was unique to that situation or what would be a more universal application. As I worked with people who had previous worked with Mr. Iacocca I also heard a repeated state that while the book is entertaining it is very biased in its view of what actually happened. Over time I have repeatedly seen that leaders who produce excellent results are unable to accurately describe what happened.*

Perhaps in summary, reading books by celebrity CEO's will make interesting reading, and may or may not be all that accurate. It is like a historical novel where the author has taken certain artistic license or privileges with details.

Conclusion

Leaders develop other leaders. Leaders guide others in skillful actions to accomplishing results. Success in execution occurs when there are leaders throughout the business. It does not happen because of one celebrated CEO or skilled site managers. It happens because of a network or team of leaders working together to make things happen that otherwise would not have happened. Developing leaders throughout the organization becomes a crucial step in successful execution.

Foundational Leaders

About the Author: Robert Chapman, Ph.D.

Bob is an expert in strategic execution or the successful implementation of strategic change. His focus in strategic execution is shareholder value creation through bold leadership, collaborative approach to management, and engagement of employees to achieve unprecedented results. Bob assists clients to achieve value creation through a blend of projects for improvement, organic growth, and external growth through acquisitions/alliances.

His specialization includes: Design of strategic execution initiatives, leadership, executive coaching and executive team formalization and functioning.

Bob has been a Partner in King Chapman & Broussard, Inc. Management Consulting Group for more than 25 years. He has worked extensively with boards of directors and executive groups. Because of his unique expertise, Bob has worked effectively with global and multinational companies in Asia, Canada, Europe, Latin America and the US. He has worked in a wide array of industries included automotive, building materials, energy, finance, forest products, mining and holding companies.

Bob received a Ph. D. from the University of Texas at Austin, a M.S. from University of Texas at Arlington and a B.A. from Howard Payne College.

4288805

Made in the USA
Charleston, SC
23 December 2009